A NATION DESTROYED

A NATION RESTORED

Inspirations from the book of Nehemiah
And Comparisons to the Rebirth of a
Godly Modern Day America

© 2010 by Arthur A. Dean

Photography of fireworks by Abigail M. Dean
from Columbus, Ohio Red, White and Boom
4th of July Celebration

Ballad of Nehemiah (chapter one)
Words By Arthur A. Dean

Scriptural quotations are taken from the New American Standard Bible.
© Thomas Nelson Publishers 1985 Edition

TABLE OF CONTENTS

NOTES:

INTRODUCTION

We live in extraordinary times in America. We have far too many politicians and very few true statesmen. We have far too many 'spiritual gurus' of all faiths and very few leaders who truly understand the concept of servant leadership. There are too many self-centered entertainers who crave being an image to be worshiped rather than being a genuine role model worthy of being emulated. News reports inform us of yet another corporate executive who has ripped off millions of dollars from their company while we ask, "Is there any business leadership left that understands customer service and knows how to truly take care of those under their charge." There are more educational institutions I care to mention that are more concerned about indoctrinating students than providing a true atmosphere of healthy debate. As a result of all this the United States is suffering from a variety of cancers, that if not treated NOW, the prognosis will not be good. These cancers have invaded our politics, our economy, our educational systems, our businesses, our entertainment / news media, and unfortunately our religious / spiritual environments.

Why am I writing this book? Let me put it this way. A conservative talk show host I listen to often presents a challenge. That challenge is that we should get on our knees and ask God what we should do in times like these. I believe that as a result of spending time in prayer and searching out truths of the Bible we can find answers and direction. I believe there is hope in spite of the housing market going sour. I believe there is hope in spite of historic levels of unemployment and national debt. There is hope in spite of purposeful government intrusion into almost every aspect of our lives. There is hope even though our economic system is hanging by its fingernails over a cliff of potential total collapse. I believe there is hope in spite of the years of indoctrinations in our educational institutions that have purposely derailed us from what our founding fathers intended. Is realizing that hope going to be easy? Absolutely, not. Let's not be in denial. Any cancer that has progressed to stage 4 requires radical treatment. When will that hope be realized? That is very, very hard to say. We have a lot more to go through until we get there. Sometimes the darkest hour has to come before the dawn. Can it be achieved? Absolutely, yes, yet not without some very difficult, painful choices. The first question is how. A second question is do we as the American people have the guts to accept those hard choices and do what is necessary to achieve that hope. A third question is will the type of *servant* leadership come forward to facilitate the direction needed to achieve that hope. (I don't mean 'political' leadership. We have had too much 'politics as usual' for far too long.)

For answers to these questions we look to a person and a society from another time and another place. We look to a genuine leader from the Old Testament. We look to Nehemiah. We look to the remnant of a people whose nation was utterly destroyed by an invading army. We look to an amazing story of how an inspired people rebuilt their lives within *52 DAYS*. We look to this story for lessons that will tell us what we can *practically* do to restore what we once had as a nation.

NOTES:

CHAPTER ONE: CELEBRATIONS

"The night had an eerie silence
As I rode up the hill.
My horse stumbled in the darkness
As I cried out to know Yahweh's will.
The walls around me had been broken down.
Not much of them remain.
My spirit broke down with tears
From the weight of the people's pain.
I tried to guide my horse backup the steep hill.
There was not much room for it to pass.
At least I could say that I was in my homeland at last."

It had been several months since those thoughts had come to mind. Who was I, Nehemiah, to be here among my people to encourage them to rebuild? Who was I, Nehemiah, a mere servant, to stand before King Artexerxes to ask for all that was needed for this work? Yet, here I was in Jerusalem, the City of King David. It was now time to celebrate all the work that had been done.

I now once again rode my horse around the edge of the city before the day's celebrations began. This time there was room to ride. The rubble had been removed. I said to myself, "Aha, Sanballat, we *were* able to revive the stones from the heaps of rubbish. Aha, Tobiah, even a thousand foxes cannot now leap the heights of the rebuild wall. We feeble Jews, as you have called us, *have* seen the impossible happen. We *are* now fortified against you. We *will* offer our sacrifices, just as days of old." Yes it was now time to celebrate.

I saw stirrings among the sentry campfires as I rode around the wall. These were not the men clad in the bronze armor and helmets of Artexerxes battalions. My eyes met with one of the men's eyes from the campfire. I reached down as I passed. Our arms clasped. No words needed be spoken. He looked back with appreciation. His rough-cut hair and graying beard gently swayed in the breeze as the sun began to rise over the trees. I made my way from campsite to campsite. There was laughing and cheerful chatter among the men such as had not been for some time. Looks of appreciation from the men's eyes met with mine.

My mind reflected on the faces seen that morning. Was not the bearded one a simple farmer from whom I had purchased grain just a month ago? Was not his friend beside him one from whom I had purchased lamb to re-supply our food? No, it was I who returned my looks of appreciation. It was because it was they and their brethren who had done the real work of rebuilding. It was people like Eliashib and the people of Jerico. It was Hanon and the residents of Zanoah who repaired the Valley Gate. They rebuilt it and put its doors and bolts and bars in place. They repaired 500 yards of the wall as far as the refuse gate. Too many people's names and faces came to mind as my eyes teared with emotion. The night of eerie silence this new morning had given way to cheerfulness and laughter. Yes, it was time to celebrate.

Later in the morning I made my way to the open square in the front of the Water Gate. I wondered who would come to the celebration. Many of the people had already settled in their own cities. Would they return? I was met with an overwhelming sight as I rounded the corner to enter the square. The square was already packed with people. The numbers were beyond the ability to count. I bent down on one knee and raised my arm in praise to Yahweh.

"All the people had gathered as one man at the square which was in front of the Water Gate, and they asked Ezra the scribe to bring the book of the Law of Moses which the LORD had given to Israel. Then Ezra the priest brought the law before the assembly of men, women and all who could listen with understanding, on the first day of the seventh month. He read from it before the square, which was in front of the Water Gate from early morning until midday, in the presence of men and women, those who could understand; and all the people were attentive to the book of the law. Ezra the scribe stood at a wooden podium, which they had made for the purpose. And beside him stood Mattithiah, Shema, Anaiah, Uriah, Hilkiah, and Maaseiah on his right hand; and Pedaiah, Mishael, Malchijah, Hashum, Hashbaddanah, Zechariah and Meshullam on his left hand. Ezra opened the book in the sight of all the people for he was standing above all the people; and when he opened it, all the people stood up. Then Ezra blessed the LORD the great God. And all the people answered, "Amen, Amen!" while lifting up their hands; then they bowed low and worshiped the LORD with their faces to the ground. Also Jeshua, Bani, Sherebiah, Jamin, Akkub, Shabbethai, Hodiah, Maaseiah, Kelita, Azariah, Jozabad, Hanan, Pelaiah, the Levites, explained the law to the people while the people remained in their place. They read from the book, from the law of God, translating to give the sense so that they understood the reading.

"This Day Is Holy"

Then I, Nehemiah, who was now the governor, and Ezra the priest and scribe, and the Levites who taught the people said to all the people, "This day is holy to the LORD your God; do not mourn or weep." For all the people were weeping when they heard the words of the law. Then he said to them, "Go, eat of the fat, drink of the sweet, and send portions to him who has nothing prepared; for this day is holy to our Lord. Do not be grieved, for the joy of the LORD is your strength." So the Levites calmed all the people, saying, "Be still, for the day is holy; do not be grieved." All the people went away to eat, to drink, to send portions and to celebrate a great festival, because they understood the words, which had been made known to them.

Feast of Booths Restored

Then on the second day the heads of fathers' households of all the people, the priests and the Levites were gathered to Ezra the scribe that they might gain insight into the words of the law. They found written in the law how the LORD had commanded through Moses that the sons of Israel should live in booths during the feast of the seventh month. So they proclaimed and circulated a proclamation in all their cities and in Jerusalem, saying, "Go out to the hills, and bring olive branches and wild olive branches, myrtle branches, palm branches and branches of other leafy trees, to make booths, as it is written." So the people went out and brought them and made booths for themselves, each on his roof, and in their courts and in the courts of the house of God, and in the square at the Water Gate and in the square at the Gate of Ephraim. The entire assembly of those who had returned from the captivity made booths and lived in them. The sons of Israel had indeed not done so from the days of Joshua the son of Nun to that day and there was great rejoicing. He read from the book of the law of God daily, from the first day to the last day and they celebrated the feast seven days, and on the eighth day there was a solemn assembly according to the ordinance." Nehemiah 8 NASB

The People Confess Their Sin

"Now on the twenty-fourth day of this month the sons of Israel assembled with fasting, in sackcloth and with dirt upon them. The descendants of Israel separated themselves from all foreigners, and stood and confessed their sins and the iniquities of their fathers. While they stood in their place, they read from the book of the law of the LORD their God for a fourth of the day; and for another fourth they confessed and worshiped the LORD their God." Nehemiah 9:1-3 NASB

It was another open square, another time, and another crowd. Images of thousands of people could be seen in the reflection pool at the National Mall. It was again another time to celebrate. This time it was a remembrance of another nation seeking to follow the God of the Scriptures. The tall monument at the end of the reflecting pool stands as a reminder of another leader, another horse ride and another time.

The general made his way through the deep snow. The wagon behind him was loaded with blankets made by his wife and as many supplies as he could gather. His eyes were met with appreciation as he made his way from tent to tent to distribute the much-needed blankets. He wished he could do more. After all, it was Christmas. His men had sacrificed much more than should be expected. They sorely missed their families. It would not be much of a Christmas. The battle had been too long. The fight had been too hard. The outcome had been uncertain. Their tents barely kept out the biting cold. Many had no shoes. Frostbite had already claimed many extremities. Stabbing hunger and tiredness only aggravated their depressed spirit. The comfort and presence of their leader, General George Washington coming to Valley Forge with much needed supplies lifted their spirits.

Yes the view of the Washington Monument is a reminder of those at Valley Forge and others who have sacrificed to establish and preserve the victory that ultimately came. The celebration at the Washington mall in August 2010 appropriately honored all who have gone before to protect and sustain that vision long ago established for our nation. The reading of our founding documents, the singing of patriotic hymns, the prayers for our nation that went heavenward and the presentations of stories of our national heroes in some ways mirrored the celebrations of Nehemiah's day. We the people of the United States also have reason to celebrate. No other nation has provided the opportunity for so long a time for the common ordinary citizen to excel.

Yet, we have not been without our challenges. Are we at the sunset or the sunrise of our history? I believe that in the new sunrise of our history we have yet many more celebrations of our national heritage. Just as Nehemiah and the people of his time overcame the obstacles to renew their faith, traditions, recalled their heritage, and celebrated their victory, we too as a nation will find a new sunrise in our history as we learn from their example.

CHAPTER TWO: OUR SITUATION

"Now it came about in the month of Chislev, in the twentieth year, while I was in Susa, the capital, that Hanani, one of my brothers, and some men from Judah came; and I asked them concerning the Jews who had escaped and had survived the captivity, and about Jerusalem. And they said to me, "The remnant there in the province who survived the captivity are in great distress and reproach, and the wall of Jerusalem is broken down and its gates are burned with fire." Nehemiah 1:1 – 2

There are keys words and phrases that stand out to me that reflect what we are experiencing as a nation. We must first recognize these concepts, and not be in denial if we are to move forward.

The first phrase is mentioned twice. That phrase is "survived the captivity". We as a nation unfortunately are held captive to many influences. For years our educational system has been held captive to humanist philosophies that denies debate. Many in the system say that there is no discrimination, yet Christian after Christian, student and professor alike have been denied the right to express their creationist views. History lessons have been 'creatively' re-written so that today's students have no clue to our historical Judeo / Christian heritage. Teachings within many business colleges berate our free capitalist enterprise system, and flaunt the 'benefits' of Socialism, Marxism and Fascism. As a result our government is working hard to set up a 'cradle to the grave caretaker service' in almost all areas. Never in our history have we seen a situation like we have now where the government thinks they can do a better job running multiple business sectors, such the auto, heath care and housing. Yet what has this brought us? A failed cash for clunkers program that has left dealerships closed; other dealerships that waited too long for government reimbursement; an automotive manufacturing sector that has closed down with massive layoffs; and a failing housing market tied with a banking system that relies on 'monopoly play money' printed on government presses.

One word in particular stands out from these verses. That word is "survived". Survival is a word that is on many people's minds. What will survival look like? From these verses we can see that there will be two types of survivors. The first type is taken from another word in these verses. That word is "remnant". "The remnant there in the province who survived." This is a scary concept. That suggests that only a remnant will successfully survive what is coming. This suggests that there could be total a collapse of this country in all arenas. It happened in Nehemiah's time. It happened to Rome. It happened to the Weimar Republic. We should not be so naive to think that we as a nation are too big to fail. If you think this is not the case, consider what is happening to the once strong economies in counties such as Greece, and now Ireland. The leadership in the European Economic Community has daily migraines over how to bail out the latest failing economy in yet another country. The remnant here in the US will consist of those who have enough foresight to prepare for what they might consider to be the inevitable. These will actually go through the tough economic times and come out on the other side. The second type of survivor will be those who do all they can to *prevent* the inevitable. These are people such as the 'Tea Party" and other individuals who are not afraid to speak out, to peaceably protest, to write to and visit congressmen, those who work hard to initiate *effective* legislative change, who don't make it a lifestyle to live on government handouts, who start their own businesses, who reach out to their neighbors and help others survive without government help. Unfortunately if this is not done, we *will* be left with only a remnant. Sadly if this is not done, there will be those who will not successfully survive.

Another phrase from these verses is, "are in great distress and reproach". Without a doubt, many in this country, myself included, are in great distress. Just recently before deciding to write this book, I was informed at work that after many years existence as a major electronics service lab, our division would be closing. I had been employed there for 11 years as a QA inspector. We were given approximately 6 months to transition all operations to an out of state facility before ours closed. Never mind that our service lab had won award after award for outstanding work. Never mind that our service lab had proven to be the *most* (in fact the only) profitable facility within our entire national chain. Never mind that we had the most qualified, hard working employees in the country. Never mind that we for years had been a showcase service lab. Never mind that we did all we could to cut costs including a cut in pay just to survive. Never mind that some employees had been with the company 30 plus years. I don't say all this out of bitterness, but as a statement of fact to what is happening to many decent hard working Americans today. I am very thankful for the time and experience I had while employed with this company. It gave me many skills I can transfer to other employment. However, there is a stark reality in existence in today's America. We've awakened to a new America where the norm is no longer 'hold onto a job for 25 years and expect a good retirement from that'. It is also no longer simply a matter of qualifications that helps one hold on to employment. As we were told, "Please don't take this closure personally. You have all contributed much to the success of our company. It is simply a business decision. It is felt that the cost of having multiple locations is too much, and therefore all operations are now being handled by our out of state facility to cut costs." How often has this line been heard? "Your job has now been transferred overseas for cost cutting purposes."

I had one of two choices given this situation. I could either become bitter or better. I could either slump down into depression or I could do what it takes to be a survivor. I chose the later. During the transition time I chose to seek out further education and job skills in another field that had a higher hiring rate with higher pay. I chose to use the cash from my separation agreement to pay down as much debt as possible and to fund getting more education and new job training. Believe it or not, I bought a new home, making use of the first time homebuyer's credit. I chose the route of becoming more independence and self-sufficient. I've decided to do car repairs myself, (since I am mechanically inclined and have a degree in agricultural mechanics) rather than pay through the nose for others to do it. I've decided to become more connected with people, to volunteer at church in the children's ministry. My wife and I planted a garden. She started a home-based business through telecommuting and other Internet opportunities. I looked at my previous successful skills and started a few things on the side to bring in additional resources. I decided to write this book to encourage others. I decided to become involved contacting my congressmen tactfully making my opinions known. Yes, our family is in very a stressful situation because of this transition. I DECIDED TO MOVE FORWARD! I'VE DECIDED THAT *I* AM RESPONSIBLE FOR MY ULTIMATE SUCCESS, NOT THE GOVERNMENT, NOT SOME SOCIAL AGENCY, NOT ANYONE ELSE. I'VE DECIDED TO DO WHATEVER IT TAKES TO BE A SURVIVOR!

Another word in the phrase "great distress and reproach' is the word reproach. Other words for the word reproach relevant to our historical times are words such as 'censure', 'accusation' and 'criticism'. Nehemiah was the type of leader (and oh, that there might be more of his type in existence in our time), who knew the cost of doing and saying what is right and ending up on the receiving end of harsh criticism, rebukes and censure. There is but a handful of individuals within our media today who really gets the message of this book. I listen to their talk shows every day on conservative talk radio. They are working very hard to get their message out and to get people to wake up to turn this country around. You know who you are, and THANK YOU. THANK YOU! If I could help wake more people up and help more people be survivors through the writing of this book, then it is well worth the effort. But, I know, as do others who are working towards the same goal, there is the cost of harsh criticism and censure. Those of the liberal bent for whatever reason do not align themselves with or are not honest about the truth of all that is happening in this country. They hatefully reproach those who do speak the truth. I will later in this book get into more of the specific accusations Nehemiah faced in his day, how he specifically responded and we can relate it to our time.

"and the wall of Jerusalem is broken down, and its gates are burnt with fire." Nehemiah 1:3

Just as the broken wall existed in Nehemiah's day, we also find that there is much that is broken in our nation. As a result just like the gates of Jerusalem, which were burnt with fire, there is much that has been destroyed in our nation. For one, our defenses against the forces that have changed our country have been down for far too long. There has been much discussion as to why we as a national defense strategy do not close our boarders and deal with the illegal immigration situation effectively. While many potential attacks have been stopped, what scares me is what we don't know, and what might already still be here because we have not closed our boarders. Our economy is also broken. The housing, health care, educational and many other arenas need major work.

This chapter paints a bleak picture and asks some serious questions that we *must* find answers for. I believe that we can learn a direction from the experiences of Nehemiah from the Old Testament. Read on . . .

NOTES:

CHAPTER THREE: OUR FIRST RESPONSES

"Now when it came about that I heard these words, I sat down and wept and mourned for days; and I was fasting and praying before the God of heaven." Nehemiah 1:4

I can imagine the crushing spirit that came over Nehemiah as he heard the report about Jerusalem. His legs gave out from under him as he listened to his brothers and friends. He could do nothing at first but sit down. How often do we rush, rush, rush trying to figure out how to handle situations, when we really need to STOP and just sit, weep, ponder and pray. Yes there is a time to build, but often it first requires a time of grief and prayer. We need to take time out and be quiet to hear from God during times of difficulty. Grief took over his spirit for days. He did the only right thing as his first response. He prayed and fasted. What he prayed also had tremendous significance for his and our time.

"And I said, "I beseech Thee, Of Lord God of heaven, the great and awesome God, who preserves the covenant and loving-kindness for those who love Him and keep His commandments." Nehemiah 1:5

Nehemiah came first to God on God's terms. It started first with really knowing who God is: "Lord of heaven, the great and awesome God". We cannot accomplish God's purposes until we first know what God's character is like. (See Daniel 11:23 "The people who know their God will display strength and take action.") We must first learn what values and principles God has and make them our own. That is what made the founding of our country so unique.

Second, we need to understand God's way of doing things. He is a God of grace and mercy "who preserves the covenant and loving-kindness for those who love Him and keep His commandments". I believe that the God of the Old and New Testaments is a God who is very willing and capable to bring restoration and renewal many times over. He is One who remembers His covenant with His people. We can only experience the practical outworking of that as we grab hold of His principles and commandments as outlined in the scriptures. Only *after* remembering God's character and a willingness to pursue truths as outlined in God's commandments and covenants did Nehemiah place his requests before God.

Third, we need to individually and corporately confess *our part* in how we individually may have gotten off track (I need to balance the next couple paragraphs with the following statements with the following disclaimer: I say '*our part*', because many in the general population are waking up and have done what is talked about in the next few paragraphs. They are getting back on track with rediscovering values and principles as outlined in scriptures. They are speaking out respectfully against what they see happening. The difficulty they are encountering though is the fallout of a corrupt and unprincipled government that has lost its way.) Nehemiah went on to say in his prayers: "I and my father's house have sinned. We have acted very corruptly against Thee and have not kept the commandments, or the statutes, or the ordinances, which Thou didst command, Thy servant Moses. Remember the word which Thou didst command Thy servant, Moses, saying, 'If you are unfaithful, I will scatter you among peoples (nations): but if you return to Me and keep my commandments and do them, though those of you have been scattered were in the remotest part of the heavens, I will gather them from there and will bring them to the place where I have chosen my Name to dwell.'"

What is Nehemiah talking about here: Look back to Deuteronomy 4 starting with verse 25. "When you become the father of children and children's children and have remained long in the land and act corruptly and make an idol in the form of anything and do that which is evil in the sight of the Lord your God so as to provoke Him to anger, I call heaven and earth to witness against you today, that you shall surely perish quickly from the land where you are going over the Jordan to possess it. You shall not live long in it, but shall be utterly destroyed. And the Lord will scatter you among the peoples, and you shall be left few in number among the nations where the Lord shall drive you. And there you shall serve the gods, the work of man's hands, wood and stone, which neither see nor hear, nor eat or smell."

Let me ask a few uncomfortable, pointed questions. Do you think that God is angry at what is happening in America today? I have mentioned briefly about the grace and loving-kindness of God. Yet, not enough is said about God's other side: His wrath and anger. Given what is happening in America today, which side of God's character do you personally want to be on? I can assure you that God is not neutral, and He will expresses His character . . . eventually. Which side of that expression do you as a reader want to be on?

Think about the consequences of forgetting God as outlined in these verses from Deuteronomy. First, there seems to be a connection between longevity of a nation and forgetting the founding roots. If each succeeding generation is not re-educated as to their roots, any country *will* fall apart and any country *will* pursue other directions. "When you become the father of children and children's children and have remained long in the land and act corruptly and make an idol in the form of anything and do that which is evil in the sight of the Lord your God..." There are consequences of that. The first is a response from God. You will, as the verses state: "provoke Him to anger". The second consequence is one that could potentially happen quickly. "You shall surely perish quickly from the land where you are going over the Jordan to possess it. You shall not live long on it, but shall be utterly destroyed." This consequence frightens me. Up until now we have been able to stop any further terrorist attacks since 9/11. God's hand and a very sharp intelligence community have stopped such attempts. But, if we don't grab hold of our roots, if we don't turn around and remember who we are under God's direction, who is to say that God would not remove His hand from the situation and allow us to experience the consequences. Who is to say that there might be a slip up in our security networks and things get through and are unleashed in this country that are far worse and widespread than 9/11 ever was. (I don't know of anything specific, but what I don't know and what I think our security might not yet know that could already be here concerns me.) Even if this does not happen, another consequence is that we as a nation could end up not achieving our fully intended potential. We could potentially not 'possess' our founding fathers' ideals. ("where you are going over the Jordan to posses it.")

Let's be honest. Do we want to become a servant to another philosophy and lifestyle other than what our founding fathers intended? If we don't turn around that will be the final consequence. "and there you will serve gods, the work of man's hands, wood and stone, which neither see nor hear, nor eat nor smell." Do we really want to serve under the philosophy 'Workers of the world, unite"? Do we want to end up where we have no voice, where our work means nothing other than serving a godless, uncaring government? Basically the only alternative if we don't turn around is to become a servant to a godless dead society based on socialism, humanism, even worse, potentially fascism or communism. Don't think it has not happened in the past. How many REPUBLICS in past human history have gone through this exact same process? How many practically empty churches exist in Europe today that are simply architectural spiritually dead reminders of times past of a nation who forgot God. How many cultures in human history have fallen from within? If the natural process of national and societal decay has happened so many times, pretty much without fail, why would we think we are any different? Are we any bigger than any other nation who has gone through this? We should not lull ourselves into slumber and think we are too big to fail.

As I see it from these verses in Deuteronomy, there are two and only two alternatives that face us. We can either turn around NOW as a nation and truly experience God's intended grace, or we can go on, experience the consequences and pain, be left with "fewer people in number"; prayerfully come out on the other side with a lot of damage, and for those who remain experience God's 'in spite of' grace.

Allow me to make this on a more personal, perhaps uncomfortable level. I have seen through the years as a Christian many people who seemed to have walked for a long time with the Lord who 'suddenly' stop that walk and go into unimaginable things. Their life now is so contrary to the life they once lead. I can assure you that in every case behind the scenes it was not a 'sudden' process that got them to where they are now. They allowed small erosions to their faith through the years grow into torrents of uncontrolled decay to the point where it is really hard to tell the difference between them and a non-Christian. Even the Apostle Paul feared that he could become disqualified from service after walking with the Lord. Am I implying that one could lose their salvation? No I don't believe in that. I simply believe that if a person does not guard over their heart and life, and allows negative thoughts, attitudes and influences go unchecked; their life's effectiveness for the faith will end up being destroyed. In fact their life in general could end up being destroyed.

Should the later of the two choices occur ether on a personal or national level, there is a direction indicated from these verses. It is a painful direction, but never the less a direction. "When you are in distress and all these things come upon you, in the later days, you will return to the Lord, your God and listen to His voice. For the Lord is a compassionate God; He will not fail you nor destroy you nor forget the covenant with your fathers which He swore to them."

Allow me to share an example as a parent the principles outlined here. My son as a teenager had a habit of wanting to ride his 10-speed bike to a convenience store after dark. He did not want to heed my warnings of going out after dark to a location that even I was uncomfortable driving to after dark. For one, he did not have any lights or reflectors. Secondly I did not trust the type of characters who showed up as regular customers. After repeated warnings, I told him that I loved him, I warned him, but I would need to allow him to experience the consequences (much to the vexation of my wife.) He came back a short time later with his leg and foot all banged up, and his shoe off. I asked him what happened. He said that somehow he got his foot caught in the spokes of his bike and took a tumble. Was I angry with him? Yes. Did I forget that he was my son? No. Did I forget that I loved him? No. Did I forget that I had warned him something could happen in the dark? No. Did I stop giving him direction in his life? No. Did he experience pain? Yes. Did he get injured? Yes. Did he learn? Yes. Would I have preferred that he listen ahead of time and not learn in the way that he did? Yes. You see, God is the same way. He sees that we as a nation are headed out into the dark. He does not trust many of the characters leading this country today. It is not because many in leadership have forgotten our roots. It is because there are those who reject our foundational principles in favor of another perspective. They are doing all within their means to steer in another direction our founding fathers never intended. God is trying to warn us of the dangers. He wants us to make the right choices. He wants us to avoid the consequences of bad choices and direction. Will He be angry if we make the wrong choices? Yes. Will there be damage if we make the wrong choices? Yes. Does He prefer that we listen ahead of time? Yes. Will He forget our past, the principles and values and covenants upon which our nation was founded? No. But He will be tremendously heartbroken that we did not listen and we go through experiencing the consequences. I believe that He is a God Who, on the other side, can bring healing and we can once again experience His love, but in a different way. It would be an 'in-spite-of' love. Just as my son's leg and foot healed, and we moved on in our relationship, so too we as a nation can be healed, but why go through the process of wrong choices to get there?

"For the Lord your God is a compassionate God; He will not fail you nor destroy you nor forget the covenant with your fathers which he swore to them." Deuteronomy 4:31.

Finally Nehemiah's initial responses involved his knowledge of who he was in God's perspective and his place in the world he knew. He describes himself as a servant of God first then lists his occupational title second. This approach has saved me many an identity crisis. I view myself primarily as a Christian first who happens to have been involved within many arenas. Each arena of life has a season, but my Christianity does not change. For a season I was a college student. That changed. I have had many places of employment. Each had a season and was an arena of involvement. I am a member of my immediate family (with my parents). My mother is now deceased and my father is in an assisted living situation. That became a new season involving change. My current employment is changing through no fault or choice of my own. The Lord is going to continually lead me into new roles with new responsibilities. I keep encouraged knowing that I am first a Christian and second that the Lord for whatever reason will continue to shift me into new arenas throughout my life. Nehemiah is about to find his roles and responsibilities change dramatically. "Now I was a cupbearer to the king." Nehemiah went from being a servant (as a cupbearer) to the king in Babylon to become a servant of the people in Judah as governor. He went from being an ordinary person in a secular role to become an outstanding servant leader who affected an entire nation. There are many biblical examples of this: Joseph, Daniel, Abraham, Moses and the 12 disciples to name a few. I say this to encourage you the reader that you should not take lightly your present role. Be faithful where you are with all the attributes of a servant. Grab hold of the vision God places in your heart within your context. Know who you are in God's eyes. Your role or position may or may not change. You, however, with a servant's attitude, can affect more people than you think, as you prove faithful to what God has placed before you.

NOTES:

CHAPTER FOUR: BEGINNING CHALLENGES AND INSPIRATIONS

It is not really revealed in the book of Nehemiah how long Nehemiah's brother and the other men stayed to visit. I can imagine the conversations though. Nehemiah asked these men to tell him more as he sat in grief over the loss of his homeland. I can imagine these men saying to Nehemiah, "If only we could somehow come up with the lumber to rebuild the burnt gates. If only we could somehow motivate the people to get the walls rebuilt." Their 'laundry list' for Nehemiah, if you will, might have been very long. Why, though, did they come to Nehemiah. I'll bet his brother knew him well and came to say to Nehemiah, "You're the man, bro. We need you to come and help". Over the coming days, as he mulled this over in his mind, Nehemiah felt compelled that he must go back and help rebuild not only the wall, but also the morale of his people. He began to brainstorm about resources and contacts available to him as a government official. He began to piece together a potential plan. Another biblical personality had found herself in a similar situation at another time. Her name was Esther. The Jews during her time were about to be annihilated. It was no mere chance that she became the new queen. It was her time. It was also an opportunity for her to speak out and do what she could do to intervene to see her people saved.

I MUST appeal to any government officials today who will listen. Do you think it is any accident that you have been elected to your position in government? Do you not know that it is now YOUR time to be a modern day Nehemiah? Do you grieve over what is happening in our country today? Do you spend time in prayer seeking God's guidance? Do you realize how far we have come from what our founding fathers were inspired to establish? Do you realize the consequences of what will happen should we continue to go in the direction we are going? You are in a position of servant leadership where you have resources and contacts and authority to help fix what is broken in America. I would appeal to you to learn from Nehemiah's example as he helped rebuild his nation.

"O Lord, I beseech Thee, May Thine ear be attentive to the prayer of Thy servant and to the prayer of Thy servants who delight to revere Thy Name, and make Thy servant successful; today, and grant him compassion before this man. Now I (*Nehemiah*) was a cupbearer to the king (*Artaxerxes*)" Nehemiah 1:11

There are amazing concepts in these verses. One is, again Nehemiah knew his place as a person in government. Notice how many times in these first couple chapters of Nehemiah the word servant is used. Yes, he was a servant to the king. Yet he knew to Whom his service was primarily due. It was not to King Artaxerxes. He was a servant first to God. Other biblical characters also knew this as well. Joseph and Daniel, to name a couple. Second, Nehemiah bathed his brainstorming in prayer that included a healthy respect for God. He had enough of a close relationship with God that he could go to God and in a conversational style ask God for what was needed. (See also Hebrews 4:16 and "You do not have because you do not ask," James 4:3) Finally, Nehemiah made his prayers specific. "Make Thy servant successful; today, and grant him compassion before this man." God, move in the heart of King Artexerxes. (See

Proverbs 21:1) Today's prayer for us is God move in the heart of our government to move it back to where it once was.

Why was it important for Nehemiah to pray specifically that compassion be granted to him from Artexerxes? That is because the work-place culture under Artexerxes was the ultimate in the power of positive thinking. You see, no one serving Artexerxes was allowed to come into his presence with any negativity or sadness. The stiff penalty for doing so was literal execution. Secular kings ruled differently in biblical times. Ester found herself in a similar situation. When she went into appeal to her husband (King Ahasuerus) on behalf of the Jews, she her attitude was, "if I perish, I perish." (Esther 4:16) Nehemiah knew if he showed negative emotions around his boss, he could possibly be executed. Yet, he was so overcome with grief over his homeland that he knew he would not be able to control his sadness. He prayed that it would lead to an opportunity to use his influence with the king to get the needed resources instead of it leading to his execution. His prayer worked.

"And it came about in the month Nisan, in the twentieth year of King Artexerses, that wine was before him, and I took up the wine and gave it to the king, Now I had not been sad in his presence. So the king said to me, 'Why is your face sad, though you are not sick. This is nothing but sadness of heart.' Then I was very much afraid. And I said to the king, 'Let the king live forever. Why should my face not be sad when the city, the place of my father's tombs lies desolate and its gates have been consumed by fire?'" Uh, oh. Was it execution time or answered prayer time? "Then the king said to me, 'What would you request?' So I prayed to the God of heaven." (Quite a prayer of thanksgiving, I'd bet plus a prayer for boldness to ask for what was really needed.)

"And I said to the king, 'If it please the king, and if your servant has found favor before you, send me to Judah, to the city of my fathers' tombs, that I may rebuild it.' Then the king said to me, the queen sitting beside him, 'How long will your journey be, and when will you return?' So it pleased the king to send me, and I gave him a definite time. And I said to the king, 'If it please the king, let letters be given to me for the governors of the provinces beyond the River (*Euphrates*) that they may allow me to pass through until I come to Judah, and let a letter to Asaph the keeper of the kings forest, that he may give me timber to make beams for the gates of the fortress which is by the temple, for the wall of the city, and for the house I will go to.' And the king granted them to me because the good hand of the Lord was on me." (Nehemiah 2:5-8) Talk about boldness. Did Nehemiah know with whom he was talking to? Yes. He knew that the king could either execute him or grant him his wish list. He knew that this royal line was responsible for harshly exiling his people and burning down his homeland. Yet he had the audacity of faith to ask for the unthinkable. Look what he came away with. He got enough resources from the king's forest to rebuild the gates to the city. Nehemiah thought also, "And, oh by the way, king, will you help me to build a fort within the city to protect me from people like you who might want to come back and occupy us again. And, oh yes, will you help me build a house I can live in while there. And, oh yes, I know you have a lot of allies who do not like our people. They will be extremely upset (and they were as we shall see) to know that someone is going back to Jerusalem to help rebuild their defenses. So, king, would you be a reference for me among your allies (the enemies of my people) and let them know you approve so they will let me through their territory to go do this work." This corrupt king could have executed him or granted Nehemiah his entire wish list plus so much more.

May I ask you a few of questions? What is your relationship like with your boss? I am not asking what your boss is like. I am asking, "Do you have the type of integrity in the workplace that should you need to ask for something, it would be granted?" Allow me to expand this questioning a bit further. What is your relationship, your testimony like with our governmental officials as you present your appeals? I am not asking what our government is like. We all know it has become corrupt. Are you living a life of integrity as you attempt to appeal to your representatives for what is needed? Can it be said of you that there is no *legitimate* thing you could be accused of that would short-circuit your request before your governmental official? How are you approaching those in power over you? Is it with respect? Or do you come across with out-of-control, irrational, berating anger? Is your conversational style characterized by interruptions mixed with ridiculous threats? You will get nowhere with these approaches. Conversely, is your dialogue a genuine emotionally 'in control' conversation based on fact. How much genuine listening, yet respectful rebuttal of the arguments takes place? Can you respectfully make known to your appointed representative your displeasure of the way things are in this country? If you are at a rally of some sort, do you leave the premises in better shape that what you found it when you first arrived? Let's not stoop to a lower level. Let's not give any reason for not seeing legitimate grievances addressed because of inappropriate behavior or attitudes. The other side can come up with enough false accusations without us adding to the fire. Each of you as a reader must individually decide what in your estimation is a peaceable, respectful protest.

The next step Nehemiah took was to travel to Jerusalem to survey the actual situation. Along the way he did some preliminary CYA work.

"Then I came to the governors of the provinces beyond the River (*Euphrates*) and gave them the king's letters. Now the king had sent me with officers of the army and horsemen. And when Sanballat the Horonite and Tobiah the Ammonite official heard about it, it was very displeasing to them that someone had come to seek the welfare of the sons of Israel. " Nehemiah 2:10

Detractors against anyone who would pursue the truth and against those who want to restore our nation today to its original vision are very real. They have specific names. I am not going to name them here. There are plenty in today's conservative media who have had the boldness to name them specifically and back their charges with legitimate facts. I defer for the moment to those in conservative talk radio and TV to help inform you about the cast of characters who are leading us down a dark path. Listen to these conservative commentators who are exposing specific people for who they really are and what they are up to. There are unfortunately many 'Sanballats' and 'Tobiahs' in our government and liberal media today. These people are very angry against anyone who they say are 'stupid' enough to place any validity in our true

NOTES:

historical past. The agenda they wish to establish is contrary to our historical Judeo-Christian heritage. In some cases they are enraged that anyone would want to do anything to help bring us back to what we once knew.

After delivering the letters to the various governors, Nehemiah traveled to Jerusalem to personally survey the situation. "So I came to Jerusalem and was there three days. And I arose in the night, I, and a few men with me. I did not tell anyone what my God was putting into my mind to do for Jerusalem and there was no animal with me except the animal on which I was riding. So I went out at night . . . inspecting. . . . and the officials did not know where I had gone or what I had done; nor did I as yet told the Jews, the priests, the nobles, the officials or the rest who did the work." Nehemiah 2:11-16.

Once again Nehemiah bathed his brainstorming and surveying the situation with prayer. He knew that any plan of restoration would have to be God's plans, not his. What a wonderful thing to have such a close relationship with the Divine Creator to be able to converse and brainstorm with Him. Any plan of restoration of America in our time can only come from the Divine Creator. The miraculous founding of our nation was inspired. Its restoration can be no less inspired as we spend like-minded time in prayer and brainstorming with the One who lead our founders. We must allow the Divine Creator put into our minds the plans that will lead to our national restoration.

"Then I said to them (*the Jews, the priests, the nobles, the officials and the rest who did the work*), 'You see the bad situation we are in, that Jerusalem is desolate and its gates are burned with fire. Come, let us rebuild the wall of Jerusalem that we may no longer be a reproach'. And I told them how the hand of my God had been favorable to me, and also about the king's words which he (*Artezerses*) had spoken to me. Then they said, 'Let us arise and build'. So they put their hands to the good work.'" Nehemiah 2:18

What a set of verses these are: filled of inspiration and instruction. I would have loved to be a fly on the wall at that 'town hall' meeting. Notice from these verses that it was a mixture of people from all social strata. Notice also by the people's responses the end result of the type of motivational servant leadership that characterized Nehemiah. 'Let us (*the Jews, the priests, the nobles, the officials and the rest who did the work*) arise and build'. True leadership is not self-serving, but motivates others to achieve their God-given capabilities. The Apostle Paul from the New Testament had it right when he described the proper structure of leadership within the church. "And He (*the Lord*) gave some as apostles, and some as prophets, and some as evangelists, and some as pastors and teachers, for the equipping of the saints for the work of service, to the building up of the body of Christ." Ephesians 4:11, 12. Notice who does the work of service and the results are. It is the general church population, supported by the leadership. Notice from the following diagram how somehow today we have turned the leadership paradigm upside down on all levels.

MAN CENTERED STRUCTURE

Dictatorial rule, overabundance of 'external'
regulations, use of threat, intimidation
and harsh punishment for those who get out of line.

Government mandates activities.

Individuals, groups, organizations and government
become subservient to a
single authoritarian personality or small elite group.

DICTATOR

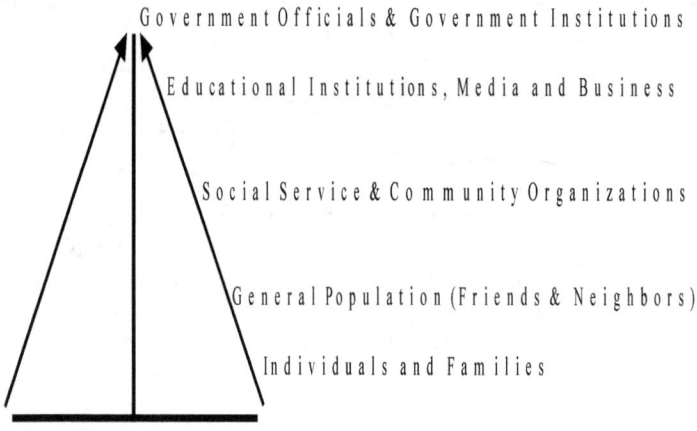

Government Officials & Government Institutions

Educational Institutions, Media and Business

Social Service & Community Organizations

General Population (Friends & Neighbors)

Individuals and Families

GOD CENTERED STRUCTURE

Servant leadership, self-rule, minimal
external rules, use of loving correction,

Acceptance, respect, forgiveness, grace and
opportunity to start over when mistakes
and getting out of line occurs.

There is self-initiative.

Servant leaders, government, organizations
and groups exist to facilitate
individuals then each succeeding level's
capabilities, which in turn promotes a
healthy society

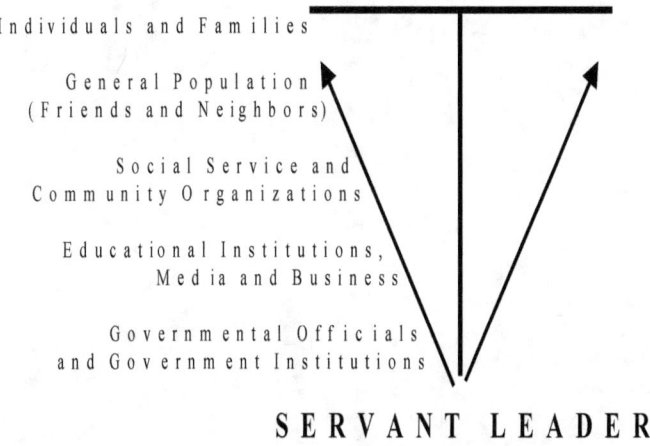

Individuals and Families

General Population
(Friends and Neighbors)

Social Service and
Community Organizations

Educational Institutions,
Media and Business

Governmental Officials
and Government Institutions

SERVANT LEADER

NOTES:

On the left side we see a man-centered structure of leadership. On the right we see a God-centered structure of leadership. On the left we see all levels of society, from individuals through the top levels of government ultimately serving a dictator. On the right we see the reverse. All organizations and institutions there, starting from the levels of government through the local social service and community organizations exist to help individuals and families to become successful. An extensive externally mandated regulatory environment characterizes the left side. The right side reflects self-rule with limited government. Was not the right side our founding father's vision? Is not the left side where many in today's politics and educational institutions will end up taking us?

How have we drifted to the left side of this picture? I believe it is because the concept of internal self-rule has slowly been replaced by government regulation and so called 'cradle to the grave' support. If a person or group cannot control themselves to do (fill in the blank), then there ought to be a law to force them to do so. I believe that due to our fallen nature as humans we have lost more and more self-control. The more we lose that, the more laws there will need to be to control bad behavior. Another way of looking at it is that there has become less and less common sense in today's society. There are some crazy laws in existence today that we would not even think of years ago because today internal common sense and self-control has been lost. To the extent that we as a society give up those two very important concepts, to that extent we are headed towards a dictatorship. Another end result is this. Individuals will also learn to turn to the government in some form for a 'cradle to the grave' support system because of the lack of internal self-control or personal initiative. The support system in today's society should properly go in the opposite direction of what is demonstrated on the left side of this chart. Support for individuals and families should come first from family, next to friends and neighbors, then to community organizations and social service agencies, then to educational institutions, media and businesses, and then LAST, to the government. What if we were to view our societal structure in this way: "And there was given to society governmental leaders, the media, educational institutions, community social service agencies and community organizations for the equipping of the general population so the general population can do the work of service to rebuild the nation." It will be individuals, families, and independently owned entrepreneurial business (whether small, medium or large) that will once again be the backbone of a re-born America. A re-born America will be one where the role of government and other institutions and organizations will be in a servant role to support, not be dictatorial self-serving entities.

"The people (*of Nehemiah's day*) replied, Let **_us_** start rebuilding' so, **_they_** began the good work." Nehemiah 2:17

"But when Sanballat the Horonite, and Tobiah the Ammonite official, and Geshem the Arab heard it, they mocked us and despised us, saying, 'What is this thing you are doing? Are you rebelling against the king?'" Nehemiah 2:19

Notice several things from the above verse. First, the cast of characters of those who oppose the rebuilding continually gets larger. This always happens when people stand for the truth.

Second: there is a denial of the facts. Of course Nehemiah was not rebelling against the king (Artexerxes). Remember that he had not only received approval from his boss, the king, he also had letters of recommendation from his boss reinforcing the rebuilding plans.

Third: Those who want to rebuild and stand for the truth will be accused of being self-serving. Look later into the book of Nehemiah where it says, "Then Sanballat sent his servant to me in the same manner a fifth time with an open letter in his hand. In it was written, 'It is reported among the nations, and Gashmu says, that you (*Nehemiah*) and the Jews are planning to rebel; therefore you are rebuilding the wall, and you are to be their king, according to these reports. And you have also appointed prophets to proclaim in Jerusalem that a king is in Judah.'" How often have we heard in today's media that those who are speaking out for the truth are only doing it for the money or are doing it to become the new leaders of a new political party, maybe even the new president?

Next there is a demeaning mocking of those individuals and groups who speak the truth. For example, it is said of the 'Tea Party crowd' that they are nothing but a bunch of uneducated, red-necked, hillbilly types. Let me tell you, I grew up dirt poor in rural Appalachia in eastern Ohio. I was able to and was the only one in my family to go to college. I have a Bachelor of Science degree. I graduated from college debt free, which is amazing because I started college with only $35 in my pocket. I have had the privilege to travel not only in Midwestern US but also abroad into a former Soviet Union satellite country to help with the church planting movement I am proud of my personal heritage and achievements, and I resent the insulting characterizations put upon intelligent people like myself who know and stand for the truth. If you want to know the truth about me, let me tell you. "Yes, I am an edjucaited red-neck who 'appens to know why we were put 'gether as a country. If you in today's gubmint and newspapers and the electronic squawk boxes (as my gran'daddy would call them) don't have a hankerin' fer that, well, that's jest tuff." Nehemiah and his people faced this type of demeaning mocking as well. "Now when it came about that when Sanballat heard that we were rebuilding the wall, he became furious and very angry and mocked the Jews. And he spoke in the presence of his brothers and the wealthy men of Samaria and said, 'What are these feeble Jews doing? Are they going to restore it for themselves? Can they offer sacrifices? Can they finish in a day? Can they revive the stones from the dusty ruble, even the burned ones?' Now Tobiah the Ammonite was near him (*Sanballat*) and he said, 'Even what they are building – if a fox should jump on it, he would break down their stone wall.'" (Nehemiah 4:1,2) We Americans are not a feeble, thoughtless, shortsighted people. We can and will rebuild, even though much has been lost! What we have done as a nation has been of great significance. What we will do again will also have great significance and positive impact. We the American people, by God's grace have excelled in our endeavors. Through that American excellence, we rank very high in terms of how much we have given out to other countries. We can revive what was once this nation, although it will be hard to go against how we have been burned by the years of the purposeful tearing down of our traditions and heritage.

Finally those in opposition to us despise and hate people like us who are educated, who know the truth and who intelligently stand for what we believe. They will do what they can to hinder or even stop the work. They will create political relationships to maneuver themselves into a position where they can cause harm. They view us as a threat to their long held offices and positions. They do not want to give up their power or position. Let's look and learn more about who the characters, Tobiah, Sanballat and Geshem were.

Tobiah was the governor of the territory of Ammon. He provoked the Ammonites to hinder Ezra's and Nehemiah's efforts to rebuild the temple and the wall around Jerusalem. (Ezra was a Jewish priest at the time who was rebuilding the Jewish temple.) Tobiah attempted to foment discontent among the Israelites so they would become discouraged and stop their work. He and his allies (Sanballat and Gershem) sent letters numerous times to Nehemiah to meet so they could 'discuss' the situation and the work Nehemiah was doing. Nehemiah was smart enough to know that they probably wanted to assassinate him, so he never met with them.

Tobiah had a close friendship with Eliashib, the Israelite high priest. Their friendship was so close that Eliashib cleaned out a room in the Israeli temple for Tobiah. To do so, Eliashib had to clean out items such as the grain used for the temple grain offering, the incense, temple articles, new wine and oil the temple workers used for their religious observances. Tobiah actually then moved his household into the newly constructed temple. When Nehemiah heard of it, he threw all of Tobiah's belongings out of what was created by the high priest as a residence for Tobiah in the temple. Nehemiah purified the room and put all the original temple items back. Imagine having to throw out a high-ranking official, a known enemy from another country, out of one of our nationally known historical landmarks.

Sanballat was a Samaritan leader and official of the Persian Achaenenid Empire. Samaritans were people who were half Israeli, half non-Israeli. There had been a long history of hatred and distrust between the Israelis and Samaritans because of the intermarriages involved. Israelis had the biblical mandate to not intermarry with ones of other nationalities. There was much distrusted of those who did so.

Geshem (who also went by the name Gashmu) lived in southern Palestine during the Babylonian exile. He had settled in or near Samaria, and was possibly closely associated with or lived near an Assyrian general by the name of Sargon. Geshem was chief of an Arabian tribe of that area.

"'So I (*Nehemiah*) answered them and said, 'The God of heaven will give us success, therefore we His servants will arise and build, but you have no portion, right or memorial in Jerusalem.'" Nehemiah 2:20.

Nehemiah knew the primary strategy of helping his people was to encourage them to do the work of rebuilding the wall. Nehemiah knew that his people were a people of promise. He kept in mind all the covenants God had given them as he pushed for the success of the project. We too as a nation are a people of promise. Our founders established many biblically based covenants. God and His principles were in the uppermost part of their minds in the early beginnings of our country. They attributed their successes to Him in the middle of incredible odds to see a new nation born that would honor and serve Him. May God also be the uppermost part of our minds and efforts are we, His servants, arise and rebuild our nation.

His *secondary* effort was to counter what his enemies threw at him. Nehemiah was discerning enough to know the difference and knew how and when to act appropriately. He knew that the goal of his enemies was to stop the work. He knew that the tools they used were discouragement, fear, demeaning remarks, intimidation, threats and false accusation. Nehemiah rightly so motivated the Israelites to keep on working and not stop because of the enemy. For us today that means that we should keep on with the positive work of rebuilding our nation. It means holding onto and promoting those values and principles that made us great. It means knowing when to rightly answer our detractors without sacrificing our primary goal of getting out the message of why we are together as a nation. "We, His servants." There have been similar phrases spoken in history that are very telling. "We the people" is one of them. "…that the government of the people, for the people and by the people" is another. This approach to governing a nation as our founding fathers established was unique when compared to what had been on the world scene for many centuries.

As for the rebuke Nehemiah gave to his enemies, he stated, "but you have no portion, right or memorial in Jerusalem." Nehemiah 2:20. Those of the socialist, liberal, progressive bent in our nation today have **no** sharing or concept of the genuine intent or principles of our founding fathers. There are probably those of that mindset that are intensely insulted by this statement. Let me respectfully ask a question. If this statement was false, why do you (of this crowd) have such a hatred of, a demeaning of and creative reinterpretation of the United States Constitution? You do have a right to express your opinions. That is granted by the Constitution you so radically oppose. *You*, however, are being *very* unconstitutional when you force us into a box of your values with the intent of eliminating our right of free expression whether it is in print, broadcast media or any other public arena. This crowd just doesn't get why we are together as a nation. And, it is Constitutionally wrong for us to be forced to join in with the 'just don't get it crowd'.

CHAPTER FIVE: THE CONTINUING WORK
AND CONTINUED OPPOSITION

"So we built the wall and the whole wall was joined together to half its height, for the people had a mind to work." Nehemiah 4:6.

How did Nehemiah organize and carry out this building project? It was a very interesting and unique example of a leader. Nehemiah in chapter three demonstrates his approach. There you will see names of individuals and groups who built their portion of the wall close to either where they lived or worked. That shows us today that the starting point for each of us exists within each of our individual frames of reference. The phrases 'and next to him' or 'next to them' or 'and after him' occurs in this chapter numerous times. The people joined forces with their friends and neighbors for mutual encouragement, support and protection. Notice also that people of all social strata joined in the work. How many priests, how many officials can you name from this chapter who helped with the work. Also how many took on the tasks as families? (Notice how many times the phrases 'their brothers' or 'the son of' is mentioned.) A small business also joined in the effort. "Malchijah, one of the goldsmiths, carried out repairs." Nehemiah 3:31.Who else from this chapter do you see was involved? It will take everyone and every business, religious and other organizations to help rebuild America. No one sector can do it alone.

Throughout the Bible we see the concept of God uniquely gifting every individual for the common good. I Corinthians 12 describes the example of the human body to make the point that all individuals within a church are necessary for a church to function properly.

"For the body is not one member, but many. If the foot should say, 'because I am not a hand, I am not a part of the body,' it is not for this reason any less a part of the body. And if the ear should say, 'because I am not an eye, I am not a part of the body,' it is not for this reason any less a part of the body. If the whole body were an eye, where would the hearing be? If the whole were hearing, where would the sense of smell be? But now God has placed the members, each one of them, in the body, just as He desired. And if they were all one member, where would the body be? But now there are many members, but one body. And the eye cannot say to the hand, 'I have no need of you.' Or again the head to the feet, 'I have no need of you.' On the contrary, it is much truer that the members that are much weaker which seem to be weaker are necessary; and those members of the body, which we deem less honorable, on these we bestow more abundant honor," " And if one members suffers, all the members suffer with it; and if one member is honored, all the members rejoice with it. Now you are Christ's body, and individually members of it." I Corinthians 12 14-23, 26-27.

The Israelites under Moses also brought their individual gifts and talents to Moses when they originally built their tabernacle in the desert. "And everyone whose hearts stirred within him and everyone whose spirit moved him came and brought the Lord's contribution for the work of the tent of meeting and for all its service and for the holy garments" Exodus 25:21. That chapter in Exodus continues to describe specific contributions and efforts the people brought for the work.

The Apostle Peter gave a directive to the New Testament church that individuals were to use their God-given talents for other's benefits. "As each one has received a special gift, employ it in serving one another as good stewards of the manifold grace of God." I Peter 4:11.

Even Jesus Christ commended individuals for making wise use of their talents while rebuking one for burying his talent. Matthew 25:14-29. Verses 28 and 29 have a lot of personal meaning to me. "Therefore take away the talent from him (*the one who buried his talent*) and give it to the one who has ten talents. For to everyone who has shall more be given, and he shall have an abundance; but from the one who does not have, even what he does have shall be taken away." I cannot tell you how many times an idea for a project has come to my mind that I did not act on. I knew that each of these specific items were things the Lord was putting into my mind to do. Yet, because of fear, laziness at the time or whatever reason I did not follow through. In every case I've witnessed someone else carrying out the same exact plan that had come to my mind. I guess that the Lord thought that if I would not follow through, He would inspire someone else. Have you ever noticed that also? It seems that the busiest people who follow through are the ones who are given more projects either through work, church, or other organizations?

There are two phrases that stand out to me from the verses in Exodus mentioned above. "And everyone whose hearts stirred within him and everyone whose spirit moved him came." Those phrases are 'whose hearts stirred' and 'whose spirit moved'. These phrases show that volunteerism for the public good is exactly that: volunteerism. Giving out to others has to be from an individual desire rather than from forced governmental regulation. The political environment today would place us under regulations that force us to give. Redistribution of wealth is a very strong concept in today's administration. Tax the wealthy to give to the poor. "The rich are too rich, while the unfortunate poor need much deserved help."

Socialism has even crept into the thinking of today's religious scene. Some in our time say, "Does not the book of Acts describe Socialism as being biblical? Should not the church follow this model?" Let's look at the verses used to supposedly support this theory. "And all those who had believed were together, and had all things in common; and they began selling their possessions and were sharing them with them all, as anyone might have need." Acts 2:44,45. The argument goes on that did not Annanias and Sapphira die because they did not share their wealth with others in the church? (Acts 5:1-10) No, the issue was not that they did not share. The issue was that they lied about how much they shared from the sale of their property. They could have shared any amount that they so desired, and that would have been OK. They wanted to make themselves out to be more spiritual by saying that they gave all from the sale of a piece of property. They were not honest in their accounting. That was the issue.

Would someone please explain to me from these verses where it says that there was a papal by-law established where they *were forced* to sell and give. The main action words in these verses are *'were sharing'*. These people were doing it out of a heart-felt willingness, not a socialistic regulatory mandate. It would be much better for us to be able to share with ones in need out of a personal willingness, rather than to be taxed and have the government ineffectively share with ones in need.

I describe the people lead by Nehemiah as 'wall builders'. They had a mind to work. Families and individuals helped to rebuild their section of the wall close to their homes and businesses. Today there are many wall builders who have a mind to work to help restore this country. These individuals have not waited for the government to inspire them *or* fund their efforts. These individuals have rallied people around them to join in projects to meet people's needs. In the conclusion section of this book are stories of these modern-day 'wall-builders'.

Let me be very clear about the approach we should take to see victory. Enemies exist that would destroy everything we have established as a country and similarly free countries around the world. It used to be that our enemies were outside the geographical United States. The free world in the past struggled against much in the world wars. We sent many dedicated service men and women into those theaters as well as later conflicts to protect and preserve freedoms for oppressed peoples. The internal conflict came to our shores on 9/11. We now find a different enemy within. President Barak Obama made a startling statement when he said, "we are now within 5 days of fundamentally changing this country". He also said if we want to know what know what he believes, then we should look to those he closely associates with. We can really tell exactly the truth of his beliefs by the socialist, communist and progressive close associations he has either through the various 'czars' he has appointed or other close advisors. What should our response be? Look to Nehemiah 4:15 for the answers.

"Now when it happened when our enemies heard that it was known to us, and that God had frustrated their plan, then all of us returned to the wall, each one to his work." Nehemiah 4:15

The most effective approach against a person or group who is deceived and wants to force their deception onto others is to educate oneself and others with the truth. The current administration and liberal media do not know what to with those of us who know the truth and are exposing them for who they really are. "When our enemies heard that it was known to us' is the phrase that stands out to me. Read books like Common Sense and Arguing with Idiots. Share these with others.

A prayer strategy for us is that God would intervene and frustrate their plans. Specifically we could pray that there would not be enough votes for bad legislation to pass in our government. We could pray against their strategies of making up the rules as they go (i.e. making the vote a simple majority to get things passes rather than their normal majority). We could pray that their coalitions would fall apart because more and more representatives begin to see the truth. We certainly have seen this type of prayer answered by the election of Senator Brown to fill Senator Kennedy's seat and the retirement of many Democrats. The coalition of Democrats and a few independents in favor of liberal legislation can become unraveled through these prayers.

Finally, our ultimate goal should always become educated about and to positively rebuild what we know to be our true founding father's intentions for this nation. "Then all of us returned to the wall, each one to his work." This phrase from Nehemiah indicates that approach.

'From that day on half of my servants carried on the work while half of them held the spears, the shields, the bows and the breastplates; and the captains were behind the whole house of Judah. Those who were rebuilding the wall and those who carried burdens took their load with one hand doing the work and the other holding a weapon. As for the builders, each wore his sword girded at his side as he built, while the trumpeter stood near him. he (Nehemiah) said to the nobles, the officials and the rest of the people, "The work is great and extensive, and we are separated on the wall far from one another. At whatever place you hear the sound of the trumpet, rally to us there. Our God will fight for us." So we carried on the work with half of them holding spears from dawn until the stars appeared. At that time I also said to the people, "Let each man with his servant spend the night within Jerusalem so that they may be a guard for us by night and a laborer by day." So neither I, my brothers, my servants, nor the men of the guard who followed me, none of us removed our clothes, each took his weapon even to the water.' Nehemiah 4: 16-23

In Nehemiah's day he felt it necessary to have armed guards protecting the work being done. That was in his day because there were enemies who would stoop to nothing to stop the work. Let me make this very clear. I am NOT advocating this approach for our time at all. We do need to be on guard, but our weapons are prayer, educating others and ourselves as to our heritage, electing and supporting people who will vote properly in supporting our true heritage and publicly 'outing' those who do not do so. We do need to have ones who 'blow the trumpet' and sound the alarm when we see anything opposed to our heritage, but I am very much against armed conflict. Our main goal is to be in support of those activities and institutions that are aligned with our founding father's true intents.

Nehemiah takes a side path in Chapter 5 on is endeavors of rebuilding the wall to deal with internal strife. There were those within Jerusalem who were taking advantage of their Jewish brethren by charging overbearing interest (usury) out of self-gain. Nehemiah puts a stop to this practice and explains how he had come to Jerusalem and was self-supporting so as to not be a burden to the people while the work went on. While I am for legitimately earned profit, may it never be said of us that we overbearingly use the situation we are in for selfish gain at the expense of others. An example I know of is this: I know of a company, which I shall keep unnamed, because it is no-longer in business, that charged an overbearing amount of fees for their financial counseling services.

They, by their practice of very persuasive presentations, placed their clients under more debt with the idea it would help get people get out of debt. Such was the practice that was occurring in Nehemiah's time. He put a stop to it and redirected their efforts to being more other's oriented.

This sidetrack of Nehemiah is another example of a servant leader. What would it be like if our government leaders were to take Nehemiah's example? I believe that the founding fathers of our country did so. As I understand it they were independently wealthy and voluntarily served in governmental leadership. Would someone please explain to me why we see some of today's governmental leaders go into office, with the designated salaries they receive, yet come out within their terms of service as millionaires? If I had their salary alone (without another source such as lobby support), I certainly could not do it. Such practices of alternate financial support for today's politicians that lines their pockets with wealth must stop! Read Nehemiah 5: 14-19 below to have a proper perspective on servant leadership.

"Moreover, from the day that I was appointed to be their governor in the land of Judah, from the twentieth year to the thirty-second year of King Artaxerxes, for twelve years, neither I nor my kinsmen have eaten the governor's food allowance. But the former governors who were before me laid burdens on the people and took from them bread and wine besides forty shekels of silver; even their servants domineered the people. But I did not do so because of the fear of God. I also applied myself to the work on this wall; we did not buy any land, and all my servants were gathered there for the work. Moreover, there were at my table one hundred and fifty Jews and officials, besides those who came to us from the nations that were around us. Now that which was prepared for each day was one ox and six choice sheep, also birds were prepared for me; and once in ten days all sorts of wine were furnished in abundance Yet for all this I did not demand the governor's food allowance, because the servitude was heavy on this people. Remember me, O my God, for good, according to all that I have done for this people."

Nehemiah 6 is a chapter that is very rich in how Nehemiah's enemies respond to the work that is progressing. They, just as today's enemies to the truth, are persistent. Lets dig into this chapter to see the progress of the work being done and the continued opposition.

The Enemy's Plot

"Now when it was reported to Sanballat, Tobiah, to Geshem the Arab and to the rest of our enemies that I had rebuilt the wall, and that no breach remained in it, although at that time I had not set up the doors in the gates, then Sanballat and Geshem sent a message to me, saying, "Come, let us meet together at Chephirim in the plain of Ono." But they were planning to harm me. So I sent messengers to them, saying, "I am doing a great work and I cannot come down. Why should the work stop while I leave it and come down to you?" They sent messages to me four times in this manner, and I answered them in the same way. Then Sanballat sent his servant to me in the same manner a fifth time with an open letter in his hand. In it was written, "It is reported among the nations, and Gashmu says, that you and the Jews are planning to rebel; therefore you are rebuilding the wall. And you are to be their king, according to these reports. "You have also appointed prophets to proclaim in Jerusalem concerning you, 'A king is in Judah!' And now it will be reported to the king according to these reports. So come now, let us take counsel together." Then I sent a message to him saying, "Such things as you are saying have not been done, but you are inventing them in your own mind." For all of them were trying to frighten us, thinking, "They will become discouraged with the work and it will not be done." But now, O God, strengthen my hands.

When I entered the house of Shemaiah the son of Delaiah, son of Mehetabel, who was confined at home, he said, "Let us meet together in the house of God, within the temple, and let us close the doors of the temple, for they are coming to kill you, and they are coming to kill you at night." But I said, "Should a man like me flee? And could one such as I go into the temple to save his life? I will not go in." Then I perceived that surely God had not sent him, but he uttered his prophecy against me because Tobiah and Sanballat had hired him. He was hired for this reason, that I might become frightened and act accordingly and sin, so that they might have an evil report in order that they could reproach me. Remember, O my God, Tobiah and Sanballat according to these works of theirs, and also Noadiah the prophetess and the rest of the prophets who were trying to frighten me." Nehemiah 6:1 – 14 NASB

Sanballat, Tobiah and Geshem used various means to try to get the work to stop. The first means was an outright scheme to assassinate Nehemiah. When that did not work their next means was to use the public press of the time, an open letter, which was essentially a smear campaign. They wanted everyone to think, again, that Nehemiah was self-serving. They wanted to portray him as wanting to be a 'king' in Jerusalem that would lead a revolution against the 'status quo' government. Ah, yes, they thought, if we could only portray Nehemiah as a 'radical revolutionary', then Artexersis will be upset and put a stop to the rebuilding effort. Nehemiah appropriately responded back to them with the truth that they were making these things up in their own imagination.

Their strategy to stop the work included intimation and discouragement hoping Nehemiah and the people would stop the work. Nehemiah's response was continued prayer for strength.

A final attempt to stop the work was to simply get Nehemiah to 'run to a place of refuge', to back off, so to speak. "Nehemiah, take a vacation. You need a break. Get out of the heat for a while. Go to a safer place. Why put all this effort into this mission. Is it worth it? You need to think of yourself and your family here. After all, it is just too dangerous to be in this type of situation where there are so many opposed to what you are trying to do. They are going to get you some day." While I believe that it is necessary to take breaks from being under the heat of opposition, it is important to be able to discern when and how these breaks should occur. Sometimes it is necessary to simply 'plow rows in the field' through the heat to hold back the fire of opposition.

Nehemiah continued his prayers by asking God to remember who those people opposing the work for who they really were and what they were trying to do. He also kept the work going in spite of all the opposition until it was done.

The Wall Is Finished

"So the wall was completed on the twenty-fifth of the month Elul, in fifty-two days. When all our enemies heard of it, and all the nations surrounding us saw it, they lost their confidence; for they recognized that this work had been accomplished with the help of our God. Also in those days many letters went from the nobles of Judah to Tobiah, and Tobiah's letters came to them. For many in Judah were bound by oath to him because he was the son-in-law of Shecaniah the son of Arah, and his son Jehohanan had married the daughter of Meshullam the son of Berechiah. Moreover, they were speaking about his good deeds in my presence and reported my words to him. Then Tobiah sent letters to frighten me." Nehemiah 6:15 – 19 NASB

It is amazing to see in today's liberal media and political arena that they do not know what to do with ones like us who have been exposing them and their strategies as we work to rebuild our nation. They do not know what to do when their political coalitions and favored legislation at times falls apart. They do not know what to do since the American populace is waking up, 'outing' and replacing progressive leaders. They are running scared about the next elections. Public denial by Nehemiah's enemies of the true facts about him did not exist in his day. Nor does public denial by the liberal media or government about the facts being exposed in Washington exist today. There is simply intimidation of the truth-speakers. We can point out what the liberal press and progressive movement is doing; yet how do they respond? Certainly it is not with any type of 'correction' by the press or those accused of what is being said. Their responses are smear campaigns, a put down of our intelligence, forming of allegiances and coalitions to circumvent the long-held legal processes in getting laws passed that we as Americans don't want and, unfortunately in some cases violence to silence their opposition. Why is this so? It is because they know we are being effective. We *are* going to win, if we just keep at it. They are running scared of that possibility. Just as Nehemiah completed the wall, so too we will rebuild this nation back to the founder's intent if we just keep at it in the proper way.

"Now when the wall was rebuilt and I had set up the doors, and the gatekeepers and the singers and the Levites were appointed, then I put Hanani my brother, and Hananiah the commander of the fortress, in charge of Jerusalem, for he was a faithful man and feared God more than many. Then I said to them, "Do not let the gates of Jerusalem be opened until the sun is hot, and while they are standing guard, let them shut and bolt the doors. Also appoint guards from the inhabitants of Jerusalem, each at his post, and each in front of his own house." Now the city was large and spacious, but the people in it were few and the houses were not built." Nehemiah 7: 1 – 4

Now that the rebuilding work was done Nehemiah did some things we should have done a long time ago. That is, 'close the gates and set up guards'.

Would someone please explain why we have not closed our boarders and set up an effective guard system? I have traveled to other countries. Going through customs is very intimidating. I know of no other country that has such open boarders as ours. We have plenty of entrepreneurial individuals and companies who could develop protective services for our boarders. Why are we not doing it? We have the know-how and technology to help us better protect ourselves. We have plenty of people who would be willing to be eyes and ears to report any suspicious activity. If anything, why not set up a citizen 'terrorist stoppers' group to use their eyes and ears to report any suspect activity? (This would be similar to neighborhood watch groups or crime stoppers hotlines.) GET ALL THIS DONE! We are only asking for trouble!

Another thing Nehemiah did was to know exactly who was in Jerusalem. He took a roll call. This perhaps might be one of the more controversial applications for our time. Do we know exactly who is here in this country and why they are here? A very bold step was taken in one of our states in the past year. It was controversial, but the Division of Motor Vehicles did not back down. Unless a person could prove they were here legally, their driver's license was suspended. This project *was* aimed at a specific group that was suspect. They complained that they were 'profiled', but DMV essentially said, "Tough luck", carried out their plan, appropriately suspended licenses, and in some cases people were deported. I make no apologies for applauding this approach. Many in this country would not want me to become president. I would not want the job either. If I were in that position, the first item of business would be to crack down hard on and deport those who are not here legitimately, close and secure ALL the boarders, and make security for ALL forms of transportation in and out of the country the strictest ever. NO ONE gets in or out without a proper security and or background check. *Everyone* must prove legitimate reason for being here or leave. Nehemiah did it in his day because of the seriousness of the dangers to their national security he knew existed. We should do the same, and make no apology for it.

CHAPTER SIX: A PERSONAL STORY

" 'For the mountains may be removed and the hills may shake, but My loving-kindness will not be removed from you, and My covenant of peace will not be shaken', declares the Lord, who has compassion on you." Isaiah 54:10

I am writing this chapter because much has changed in the America we know. Much has changed also on a personal level for many Americans. We are waking up to an America we have not known. For many the rug has been pulled out from under them either through a job loss, loss of a home and all the personal stresses that go with the events they find themselves in. The question in the back of many people's minds is, "What's next for me and my family?" In light of that I want to tell you my personal story.

A number of years ago a close friend shared some questions with me. He asked, "What would happen if you were to find that everything about your life was suddenly changed? What would happen if suddenly, to use the expression, the rug was pulled out from under you to such an extent that absolutely everything you were used to was no-longer in existence?" Then came the final piercing questions. "What would it take to 'blow you completely out of the water' spiritually, emotionally, financially and circumstantially? What circumstances would come into your life that would shake your equilibrium to the core? What would the devil have to do to get you completely off base?"

I did not want to think in those terms. I grew up dirt poor in rural Appalachia. It was a very difficult childhood. Through the years I was able to grow out of those difficulties. At the times of hearing those questions I had grown spiritually. I had build very good relationships at work, in the church and in the community. Financially I was better off than at any other time in my life. I owned my own home, had a good vehicle, and was stably employed and active in my church. The Lord had brought healing in many areas of my life. I had been able to effectively share my testimony with many people in a variety of situations throughout the Midwest through music, drama and evangelistic outreaches. I loved the Lord and was having a tremendous impact at work and in ministry. I did not want to see change. I did not want to see difficulties come into my life that would test me to the core.

Picture for the moment the scenic view of Mount Saint Helens. There was a pristine lake, gorgeous stately trees that were aflame with color every fall. It was a picture of heaven on earth. Who would not want to live there forever? Yet, in a brief moment of time that setting changed catastrophically. My friend's questions came to mind. What if such a catastrophic event or series of events were to occur in my life? I did not want to think about it.

I give credit for becoming successful to several things. A) Knowing the nature of God's attitude towards me; B) Knowing who I am and what I believe C) having friends who have stood with me in tough times; and D) Having some spiritual, emotional and to the best of my ability financial preparation done ahead of time.

My story begins in the spring of 1995. I was a very committed (sometimes over committed) person. I was working many hours as a financial consultant. My responsibilities involved counseling families who were going through hard times. I helped them to develop financial plans for emergencies and for the establishment of their sound financial future. (It is amazing that I would soon be tested in the very thing I was helping others with.) I also was very active in my church in a growing drama ministry. I had directed, performed in, wrote material for and done behind the scenes technical work for this ministry. In February of that year I was the lead in a children's musical. It was very difficult because I was drained of all energy. I had recurring abdominal cramps. My visits to the doctor were mysterious. The reports were inconclusive. The best guess was that I had chronic fatigue syndrome. Other complications showed up in test results as well. My liver enzymes one week seemed normal then tested abnormal in future tests. In the middle of this my heart started having unexplained irregular rhythms. My body was beginning to shut down, and no one knew why. This could not be happening to me at age 42.

This pattern continued until Labor Day weekend 1995. On the Monday before that weekend I experienced intense pain in my right thigh muscle. All indications seemed to indicate a pulled muscle. I treated it as such with the advice of a friend who is a physical therapist. Friends wanted me to join them for a weekend campout. I said, "We will see". Tuesday I woke up with a 102-degree temperature. My right leg throbbed worse than ever. I called my physician immediately and was able to see him the next day. From the view he got from the X-ray he scheduled an emergency appointment for me with an oncologist. My temperature hovered between 102 and 103. Headaches like I had never had in my life began to occur. Thursday morning my right leg had swollen larger than the diameter of a good-sized watermelon. Upon seeing me, the oncologist admitted me to the cancer ward of the OSU University Hospital for emergency surgery, with the word "STAT" on the report.

Finally in the emergency surgery the culprit of all my ailments was removed. A cyst had been residing and slowly growing in my leg for a long time. In the early stages my system had been filtering out its growing infection. During the spring and summer of 1995 my immune system sometimes would gain, sometimes loose. That explained the sometimes good, sometimes bad test results. Finally the cyst had grown to a monstrous size, exploded and sent its malicious poisons throughout my entire body. It affected every major system and my body was shutting down. My weight in two weeks had dropped from 140 pounds to below 100. (Not the weight loss program I would have preferred.) I can remember hearing in my sedated state some of the doctor's discussion about me. Phrases like, "If this progresses any further, he may have to have open heart surgery to repair damage to the heart valves." "We can remove the damaged muscles in his leg, but amputation might still be a possibility." Some time later after my leg surgery doctors informed me how fortunate I was, because most cases like mine that they see the patient does not survive. It was a very severe infection and if not taken care of, it could easily have turned into a more severe case. They advised me that I was fortunate. They had stopped it in time. I would not need amputation at least at the moment. I would need long-term antibiotic treatment and physical therapy. They warned me that if I did not exercise my leg properly, I could still lose it.

Could this be the situation my friend referred to in his earlier questions? Did he have a prophetic sense about me? It certainly seemed so at the time. I was in the hospital for some time and took a medical leave of absence from work to recover. I was on crutches for four months, and on the strongest antibiotics much longer than my doctor felt comfortable. If the oral antibiotics did not work, it would mean another hospital stay for IV antibiotics. I had weekly, then monthly checkups for two years, then every six months for several more years. Eventually through rehab, prayer and the help of many friends my health returned. I can exercise and do all my normal activities now, with the exception of impact sports. I took up riding a 10-speed bike. I got to a point in my recovery where I could ride 20 miles at a time and not feel tired at all. That was such a contrast to where I was when this started, where I could not walk 10 feet without feeling out of breath like a 90 year old. All the physicians had given me all kinds of potentially negative predictions of what could happen in the long term. So far, by the grace of God, none of those predictions have come true.

To top off the medical difficulties I was going through, the financial services company I was working for declared bankruptcy and closed. I was now recovering and out of work. I indeed was starting over. (I fortunately was able to find permanent employment with another company within a very short time.)

Travel with me now a little further in time to some even more intense challenges. The time was early autumn, 1999. The week had been a hard one. I had spent many late nights on various projects. The reward would come at the end of the week with a trip to one of my favorite places: Cedar Point, Ohio. As an addict of roller coasters, I loved spending time at this roller coaster capital of the world. My new place of employment had a tradition of providing an all expense (including spending money) trip there as a company outing. I said, "Are you kidding me? Let's go!" So I told my kids to get as many of their friends from church together and we would pack our van for a fun-filled day.

That Saturday morning started out with the usual hectic pace of getting everyone out the door. Finally we all piled in the van and were on our way! It was a picture perfect day of fun and thrills. By 11 PM all the rides shut down and I was really tired. As we were about to exit the park at midnight, park officials decided to start up all the rides for employees and anyone still in the park. It was a great opportunity to catch some more thrills without the long lines that had characterized the day. My wife became ill from the last inverted roller coaster ride. She asked that we give her time to recover before starting the 3-hour van ride home. By the time we all piled back into the van it was 1 am. I felt beyond exhaustion.

For those of you who know the route, State Route 4 between Sandusky, Ohio and Columbus is a long, lonely drive. This is especially true in the middle of the night. Everyone had sacked out in the van. I finally reached the intersection of Route 4 and State Route 23. At least I was now on a divided highway. The trip should go faster. The last thing I remember when pulling onto Route 23 that I was extremely tired. I was becoming more difficult to concentrate on the road. That was the thing I remember until I saw the 55 MPH speed limit sign coming directly at me right in front of the windshield. I had dozed off while driving full speed along the edge of the highway. I my dazed state, I did what is a natural reaction. I jerked the steering wheel (too much) to get us back on the road. My daughter, Abigail woke up and asked, "Daddy, what are you doing?"

It was too late to do anything else. I had overcompensated. The van began to roll over. I had lost total control. In the midst of all the screams the van bounced and crushed in one side of its roof. The front and back windows shattered. The second roll took the van down over the freeway bank into a slide and came to a stop by hitting a tree.

Abigail and her friend were hanging upside down by their seatbelts. The van had hit so hard on the passenger's side where my wife was sitting that she broke her collarbone and tore her rotator cuff. Yet, amazingly she got the kids out through the front broken windshield. She shouted to everyone to get away from the van. The motor was still running, and we smelled gas. In our shouting to get everyone away from the van we realized that our son Nate and his friend, Scott were nowhere to be found. We shouted out for them in the dark. We feared going back to look around or under the van. As we found shortly, they had been ejected through the back hatch onto the highway between the first and second roll of the van. As Scott was being ejected out the back, his leg caught on a jagged edge of the broken hatch. It made a deep, long and savage cut down the length of his shin. As we made him lie as down he began to go into shock from his blood loss.

Nate stumbled to us from the direction of the median. He had slid on his back across the asphalt through the shards of glass into the median. In his dazed state he kept mumbling the words "Raptor". He thought he had just departed from the last inverted roller coaster at the park. Blood was coming from the cuts in his skull and back. We made him sit down also to prevent shock.

Those injuries described seemed to be the most serious. I only suffered a bruised forehead from hitting the steering wheel. All other injuries were seat belt burns and bruised muscles. After seeing the van with its entire roof crushed in, and knowing that there were two ejections from the vehicle, it is amazing that no one was killed.

There were others cars on that stretch of highway that early morning. People were close enough to call for emergency help and to assist. They were not too close that anyone else was involved. And fortunately, neither Nate nor Scott was run over as they were ejected onto the highway. Amazingly in those early morning hours 2 emergency squads and 2 fire trucks were on the scene within 5 minutes of the first call for help. The officer in charge of the scene pointed out to me later that based on my tire tracks I had been asleep at the wheel for at least 4 miles.

We were transported to two different hospitals. Nate and Scott were transported to a closer one, perhaps because of their more serious injuries. The rest of us were transported to another emergency room. This was particularly distressing, because NEVER separate a mamma bear from one of her cubs. Patricia was distraught about being separated from Nate. She had a right to be. Just before transport Nate showed further signs of shock. He did lose consciousness during his trip and was in and out of that state over the next several days. During that time neither the doctors nor we knew if he would slip into a permanent coma.

We were eventually released and transported to the other hospital to where Nate and Scott were. Although Scott's wound was severe, he has made a full recovery. Nate was another story. He was still unconscious when we arrived at his hospital. Emergency personnel were picking glass out of his skull. The decision was made to transport him to Children's Hospital, Columbus Ohio for more intensive care. Over the next few days he hovered in the twilight of consciousness and unconsciousness. We were again warned that he could slip into a permanent coma. Even if he should wake up we were warned that due to his head injuries, he might never be the same. Eventually he did wake up and remained awake. Over time he has seemed fine, but we would have to watch.

There is the expression that time heals all wounds. That is not entirely true. It has taken time for us to have some degree of recovery from that accident. Nate's only remaining wound is his right toe that no longer works because of a severed ligament that could not be corrected by surgery. Patricia's injuries have been the most enduring. She had already had back problems due to spinal surgery at age 17. Over time the accident lead to further problems. Arthritis set into old wounds. Protruding disks entered the picture. Complications and further surgery came into the picture. As a result of the accident she has not able to further pursue her career as a teacher. She has not been able to sit or stand for long periods without pain. Flashbacks of the accident for some time came back to all of our memories.

Although we were fortunate to have had good insurance that paid for most medical bills plus the purchase of a new van, consequences of the accident began to send us on a downward spiral. Insecurities, anger and arguments became more intense. Insufficient income and constant calls and letters from creditors quickly eroded my self-esteem. We thought that perhaps moving to a quiet place in the country would help. It turned out to be a hasty emotional decision that was not well thought out. It was a far more expensive move than we anticipated that practically did not work out. The constant long drives back and forth to work, church and friends wore out our already shattered finances, vehicles and us. Even additional part time work did not keep pace with the overwhelming financial disaster we found ourselves in. I swore that I would never again answer the phone or go to the mailbox because of depression over bills.

The lowest point came when we met with a credit counselor. He looked over our situation and told us there was nothing consumer credit counseling could do for us that we had not already done. We had done everything right, but were just too overwhelmed. We had negotiated with every creditor. We had kept them informed. We had wheeled and dealed. We had made settlements for lesser amounts due. We had negotiated interest rates to unbelievably low levels. Credit counseling could not have done a better job. They were beginning to echo our creditors advice. Just declare bankruptcy and get it over with. That went against every standard I had ever believed in or had been taught. Yet, now it seemed there was no remaining choice. Finally after much painful struggle, research, thought and prayer, we obtained an attorney and completed the process.

I say that this was the lowest point, because I had to look back to where we had come from. We lost the following A) The house I lived in and loved before we got married. I had turned it into as rental, but the tenant disappeared without a trace. I had to sell it to pay off that loan. B) The house Patricia owned before we got married. C) The first house we owned in town after our marriage, and the wonderful house we had built in the country. Patricia lost her ability to work because of ongoing medical issues. Some friends and relationships had become distant, people had changed either due to moving on to other callings or their own circumstances and trials, and some put on masks and weren't as genuine with us. D) Our vehicles had become more unreliable due to the many miles of travel.

At that lowest point the words of my friend from long ago came vividly back to mind. "How would you respond if you found yourself at a different place in life where everything you were used to had changed. What would it take to completely 'blow you out of the water' so to speak? Yes, we had lost everything. Our finances were shot. Our health was not the greatest. We were getting older. Our vehicles were junk. My career had stalled. Friends had moved on or the relationships had changed. We could not afford to live where we were, but had no idea of how to afford moving to any other place.

I said earlier there were three things that have helped me in times like these. They were A) Knowing the nature of God's attitude towards me B) a few friends who actually did stick with us C) Having a bit of emotional and spiritual preparation done ahead of time.

As to the first, I realize now that after being slammed up against the wall of circumstances with nowhere to go, with no answers as to why God would allow everything to happen as it did, and with no solutions, that my friend was actually asking the wrong questions. It was not a matter of 'How would I respond.' Or 'What would I do.' It was a matter of, well, let me change the questions by replacing the word 'I' with the word 'God'. You see, my struggles were from a failing attempt to keep things together merely on a human level. The questions became very different. What would happen if God were to find that everything about my life was suddenly different? How would He respond?

"'For the mountains may be removed and the hills may shake, but My loving-kindness will not be removed from you, and My covenant of peace will not be shaken', declares the Lord, who has compassion on you." Isaiah 54:10

I've learned that nothing and nobody can remove God's loving-kindness. NOTHING! NOBODY!

"The Lord' s loving-kindnesses indeed never cease. His compassions never fail. They are new every morning. They are new every day. Great is His faithfulness." Lamentations 3:22, NASB

"He who did not spare His own Son, but delivered Him over for us all, how will He not also with Him freely give us all things?" Romans 8:32 NASB

"Who will separate us from the love of Christ? Will tribulation, or distress, or persecution, or famine, or nakedness, or peril, or sword?" Romans 8:35

"For I am convinced that neither death, nor life, nor angels, nor principalities, nor things present, nor things to come, nor powers, nor height, nor depth, nor any other created thing, will be able to separate us from the love of God, which is in Christ Jesus our Lord." Romans 8:38 NASB

We in life, even as the best people, are not immune to intense struggles. The context of the above verses should be even more of an encouragement. They were not penned during 'rosy' times. The verses from Isaiah and Lamentations were written during the beginning of the exiles of the Jews. The verses of the Apostle Paul came from the context of his personal struggle, yet he penned the words:

"My (God's) grace is sufficient for you, for power is perfected in weakness. Most gladly, therefore, I will rather boast about my weaknesses, so that the power of Christ may dwell in me." II Corinthians 12:9

Read on . . .

"Are they servants of Christ?--I (Paul) speak as if insane --I more so; in far more labors, in far more imprisonments, beaten times without number, often in danger of death. Five times I received from the Jews thirty-nine, lashes. Three times I was beaten with rods, once I was stoned, three times I was shipwrecked, a night and a day I have spent in the deep I have been on frequent journeys, in dangers from rivers, dangers from robbers, dangers from my countrymen, dangers from the Gentiles, dangers in the city, dangers in the wilderness, dangers on the sea, dangers among false brethren; I have been in labor and hardship, through many sleepless nights, in hunger and thirst, often without food, in cold and exposure. Apart from such external things, there is the daily pressure on me of concern for all the churches. Who is weak without my being weak? Who is led into sin without my intense concern?" Romans 11: 23-29 NASB.

God is not shaken by anything that has happened in our lives. He has personally demonstrated more compassion to us than I can include in this chapter. That compassion has come through re-uniting with old friends, meeting new friends, miraculously answered prayers coming through just at the right times, being able over the long term to work through our difficult finances to again be able to buy another home, new employment prospects that came over the horizon, plus many more answers to prayers of healing.

I need respond to a question that has been asked of us by some people. We have been asked (perhaps like Job from the Old Testament). That question is, "What sin have we committed that we should go through such horrendous circumstances?" I can say with confidence that we have made some mistakes, but no sin was involved. Don't let yourself fall into that trap of thinking. Stuff in life simply happens to the best of people. I simply fell asleep at the wheel on the road on that dark, lonely night In spite of that I know beyond any shadow of a doubt that God loves my family and me.

For those of you who question this approach of faith, consider that God is a God who specializes in putting together shattered lives. Think of Joseph from the Old Testament. He did everything right in his life. Yet, he was sold into slavery and was sent to a foreign country. He made the most of his circumstances and chose to honor God by becoming a person of excellence. What did that get for him? He was falsely accused of rape and ended up in prison. He again made the most of his circumstances and pursued excellence in prison to where he was placed into a supervisory position over other prisoners. What did that get him? The prisoners he helped, when they were released, forgot about him and left him to rot in prison. Joseph's exile lasted 17 *years*. It lasted until such time as God had planned to bring him out to shine and influence an entire *WORLD* for His glory. In short, the preparation work God takes us through in any desert experience does not even compare to the fantastic work He has for us *IN THIS LIFE* after we have gone through it. Ultimately it does not compare to what He has in store in the life to come.

As to the second source of strength prepared before our trials began. I can only describe it this way. I will use an example from my work environment. At work we have designated emergency response teams. I am on one such team. I am certified in first aid, CPR and AED. I am fortunate enough as well to have a "Spiritual Response Team". I have individuals available to me (and I for them) that I can go to for spiritual, emotional, relational and financial emergency help. Such was the case during our accident and recovery period. I cannot say, "Thank You" enough for those individuals who came to our aid with meals, transportation to medical appointments and therapy sessions, or just being there. Everyone needs such a 'crisis team', because crisis will hit us all at one point or another. Yet, what do we as *'real men'* do? We try to 'suck it up' ourselves and 'pull it together' in our own strength. Let me tell you, we are in such a situation in the 'New American Scene' (brought on by the effects of the progressive movement) that we cannot be lone ranger people any longer. It just won't work.

Finally, the last preparation I should say the Lord helped me with is this. You may have noticed how much I refer to the Bible in this chapter. I have memorized countless verses and sections of scripture that have become the bedrock of my personal convictions. These memorizations have stuck with me in hard times. I am working on another book based on those memory verses. The theme of that book is "Not Loosing Hope in Tough Times". Some sample chapters are:

Keeping Hope Because of Knowing God's Love (49 Verses)
Not Losing Hope When Encountering Personal Temptation (49 Verses)
Not Losing Hope When Dreams and Visions Seem Lost (Joseph's Story)
On the Road to a Dream (The Exodus Story)
Not Losing Hope When Under Pressure and Opposition (David's Story)
Not Losing Hope When Facing When Facing Persecution (I Peter)
The Ultimate Hope We Have in Christ (The Book of Ephesians)

You see, the first thing each of us has to do to see change in our country is to make it on a personal level. We need to know first of all what we believe, why we believe it and act accordingly. We need to dig our personal roots down deep enough into valid bedrock beliefs that will withstand the circumstances that are coming our way. We next need to establish the type of relationships that form 'crisis response teams'. There are still many quality friends who will listen to your situation and stay with you in hard times. Go to them as needed. We need to look out for each other, because the government not only won't help, the government is not going to be able to help. Our government is more broken than we are. Many assistance programs often run out of funds.

Also we need to remember that God loves us and wants our restoration as individuals, families and as a nation.

Many of you reading this book are going through circumstances similar to what I have gone through. A loss of job or health has left your spirit broken; your motivation for wanting to try anything dead and your dreams and hopes nothing more than a distant clouded memory. You can no longer muster up the energy to even want to think about those any more. Need I also say that for some the thought stopping pursuing the Christian life has crossed your mind? Some of you are bitter at God and the church. If the truth were to be known, you may have cursed Him and others a time or two and the old haunts and temptations "seem" to be more profitable. Even in all of this, nothing has caught God off guard. Remember that God is a God of restoration and healing no matter how far things have gone. "Therefore He is able to save completely those who come to God through Him, because He always lives to intercede for them." Hebrews 7:25

Also remember the words below:

"'For the mountains may be removed and the hills may shake, but My loving-kindness will not be removed from you, and My covenant of peace will not be shaken', declares the Lord, who has compassion on you." Isaiah 54:10

NOTES:

CONCLUSIONS

A nation works best when individuals are free to explore their God-given talents with limited governmental interference. Our founding fathers realized this and setup such a system that was based on rugged individualism and the capability of self-rule. Any government will always take advantage of a situation of becoming more controlling to the degree a people depart from being self-sufficient and give up their capability of being self-governing. We must recapture that entrepreneurial spirit that was so evident in our early years as a nation. In that regard we must individually explore and develop the God-given skills that we can bring to the table to help restore what we once had. In a sense we each must become a 'Wall-builder". No one person, group or politician can do the task alone. We must relearn how to keep ourselves in check so that we do not have to rely on a proliferation of legislation to govern over what should be common sense behavior. We must re-educate ourselves concerning the structure and systems of checks and balances our founders set up that helped to support this type of free entrepreneurial environment. Finally we must learn how to appropriately deal with those individuals in government, education the media and business that have taken a departure from our founders' true intent.

The remainder of this section includes but a few suggestions on how to proceed. This is not an all-inclusive list, but simply a review of action statements that stood out as writing each chapter of this book. Spend some time brainstorming with others over these suggestions as well as others that may not be included.

The very first item mentioned, which Nehemiah also did, was to spend time in prayer asking God for direction. Our country in-debatably was founded on Judeo Christian principles. Any restoration should also be God-directed. Once we see restoration making headway, we should continue our prayers to keep us on track.

Part of our prayers should be that we discover and support the type of servant leadership who will come forward in ALL arenas that will help us as a population recovers our roots. These arenas should not just be politicians we feel comfortable voting for (not merely voting for the 'lesser of two evils') but also servant leadership in education, the media and business.

The personal story demonstrates that even with things going well, bad things still happen to good people. We must each not beat ourselves up too much when things go haywire. Simply learn from the experiences and work to regroup efforts. Part of the healing process that helps is knowing what you believe, why you believe it, and keeping that positive belief system in the forefront of your thinking. Memorize key belief statements so that they can come easily to mind. Don't forget what caused you to be successful in the past.

Part of recovery both individually and within our government, education, media and business is realizing what is broken, fixing what can be fixed and which you can control, and not overly fretting over, but praying about what is seems to be out of control.

On an individual basis we, must learn what it means to become and remain survivors. Part of that learning process could involve reading inspirational stories about and learning from people who have survived tough times. In our learning process we must wake more people up and help them become survivors. I need to put a disclaimer here. I am not meaning to suggest that we all run and isolate ourselves in the mountains or wilderness and let whatever happen outside our little 'survival encampment' we create. What is meant is a learning process of how to deal with economic downturns, job losses, food, energy or other resource shortages. In short we must learn how to prepare for tough times. Develop a survival plan. Include others in that plan. Develop your skills to become a resourceful person. Don't be a lone ranger, but be a part of a 'survival emergency response team' to help others and to *ask* for help when *you* need it.

Above all when wanting to see change, maintain this principle. Maintain your integrity within all arenas that you are involved in, whether it be family, employment, or communications with government officials.

Pursue and promote unchangeable truths. Be a person of principle. Verify and appropriately expose untruths. As you do so, do not fear criticism and censure.

Finally, maintain your focus on rebuilding activities instead of becoming overly distracted by countering the opposition. Become involved with 'Wall-Building' activities. Below are some examples of such activities.

Angel Food Ministries is one such project. From their web site we read: "In 1994, Pastors Joe and Linda Wingo found their hearts going out to the families of many of the local families in Monroe, GA, affected by the recent industrial plant closings. On their back porch, the first Angel Food distribution fed 34 families. Over the next years, other churches wanted to be get involved, and Angel Food began feeding hundreds of families across the southeast. Now, Angel Food feeds over 500,000 families a month in 35 states. Angel Food Ministries is a non-profit, non-denominational organization that crosses denominational lines and has spread the good news of the gospel of Christ through salvation tracts that are placed in each food order. There are no qualifications, minimums, income restrictions, or applications. Everyone is encouraged to participate. Some churches even encourage participants to apply the money they save to help someone else in need." Basically families place an order for one week's worth of food at a discounted price. The quality is very high and very reasonably priced. The orders are then packaged and shipped from the main distribution center to churches that are a part of the distribution network. http://www.angelfoodministries.com.

"Tool Slingers" is a group of volunteers within a church I attended a while back. The individuals within this group made their skills known to the church congregation. There are auto mechanics, carpenters, electricians, and many more all-around handymen (and women). They made themselves available on a volunteer basis to help anyone in need that could not afford services otherwise. Many people who found themselves in need availed themselves of their services. I know of many other churches that have similar services. One in particular offers simple car repairs for single moms. Free day care is provided for a day while simple oil changes, tire changes perhaps spark plug changes, other electrical or other checkups and other minor repairs are done.

A 'Giving Garden" has been started at the church I currently attend. Fresh vegetables are grown in this garden to add to the other items in our food pantry to help ones out in need of food.

Www.thepeopledecide.com was created to help keep people informed about current legislative activity. Contact information for every US senator and congressmen is included on this site as a means for people to expresses the views to their particular representatives. A link to each document of legislation is also included so that the public can read each original document in its entirely. An added feature on this site is a virtual voting booth so that each member to the site can say 'Yea' or 'Nay' to each piece of legislation. Each representatives voting record on the legislation is also included. These features help members compare their votes with government official's votes. Where each piece of legislation is at in the process is also indicated, whether it is just newly being introduced, up for a senate or house vote or in committee. Regular legislation alerts can be sent to member's E-mails as an option. The best feature about this site is that it is a FREE service.

Start an annual community festival that celebrates our heritage. Include with it a reading of our founding documents, prayer, worship and feasting.

If you were to be known as a 'Wall builder", what service would you provide, or what need would you fill?

NOTES:

DISCUSSION QUESTIONS:

Introduction

1   How does the author describe the extraordinary times we live in today? Do you agree or disagree, and why or why not?

2   Describe the extraordinary times Nehemiah lived in.

3   Why did the author write this book?

4   The author poses several questions towards the end of the introduction. How would you answer those questions?

Chapter One   Celebrations

1   Many of the original customs and practices were brought back into the Jewish cultural life once the wall was completed. What were some of those cultural practices and customs?

2   What are some of our cultural customs and practices that can help us remember our heritage?

3   Describe some of the particular celebrations or traditions you and your family have which help you to remember our national heritage? If you do not have any such traditions, what could you do to help celebrate our past?

Chapter Two   Our Situation

1   Four key words are used in chapter two to describe Nehemiah's and our circumstances. What were these four key words? Compare and contrast Nehemiah's and our circumstances using those four key words.

2   Describe situations you know of (without mentioning names) of people who are experiencing circumstances related to these four key words. If you are experiencing anything related to these four key words, briefly tell your story.

3   What attitudes helped the author overcome the situation when he found out he was going to lose his job?

4   There are many things that are broken in our nation today. The author mentions a few. Would you agree or disagree. Why or why not? Are there other areas that should be mentioned?

5   Take some personal private time outside of the setting of this small discussion group to do a self-evaluation. Is there anything broken in your personal life that needs mended and needs prayer. Next take some private time with your family and ask if there is anything broken and needs mended there. When appropriate, seek outside prayer and assistance.

Chapter Three   Our First Responses

1   What is the first main response mentioned that Nehemiah did and that we need to do, given the situation in our nation?

2   What must we first know before taking action? (Daniel 11:23)

3   What must we first confess in order to make progress?

4   Why do you think that the author believes that even after taking these steps that the task of restoring our nation will not be an easy task? What particular obstacles does he point out are in the way?

5   What consequences are described relating to forgetting God and our Judeo-Christian heritage?

6   Do you agree or disagree with the assessment in chapter three that should we forget God, there is a possibility God may allow us to experience the consequences of forgetting? What might those consequences be? How does the author relate this to a personal application?

7   The author describes a situation with his son where he did not want his son to go out at night to ride his bike to a store. Relate this story to how we can view God's character and attitude towards us a nation.

Chapter Four   Beginning Challenges and Inspirations

1   We obviously have many in our governmental circles who do not 'get it' in terms of why we are together as a nation. As a result they, in the author's opinion, are pushing our nation away from our founding father's intentions. What should be our attitude and behavior towards those individuals?

2   What would be inappropriate attitudes and behaviors towards those in authority?

3   What specific appeals is the author making of our government officials?

4   To whom did Nehemiah look to put together specific plans for rebuilding the wall around Jerusalem, and why? How would that apply to us today and why?

5   The term 'servant leadership' is used numerous times in these chapters. Describe the characteristics of a servant leader.

6   There is a chart included in chapter four which demonstrates two approaches to running the country. Explain the elements of these two approaches. Do you believe it is possible to get back to the chart on the right? Why or why not? What would need to take place in order to get there?

7   Who did the main work of rebuilding the wall around Jerusalem? What role did the governmental leadership under Nehemiah play? Who should do the main work of rebuilding our nation? What role should our government play?

8   Why, according to the author, has the government stepped in to take over so much authority in so many areas of our lives?

Chapter Five   The Continuing Work
                       and Continued Opposition

1   It has been said that we as citizens seem to be doing everything right. We have prayed, we have appealed, we have E-mailed, called and visited our representatives. Yet it has been said that they just are not listening. Brainstorm together on what positive steps can be taken to get our government's attention and help restore our nation back to its founding principals. What attitudes and actions should be avoided?

2   What was the main thing Nehemiah focused on with his work in Jerusalem, without avoiding a secondary focus? What was Nehemiah's secondary focus? What was the result his sticking with his primary focus? In what ways did he respond to his secondary focus?

3   In what ways did Nehemiah's enemies respond as a result of him sticking with his main focus? How did his enemies feel when they saw that the work was done in spite of all their opposition? What lessons can we learn from that for our time?

4   In Nehemiah's time they literally established armed guards to protect the work due to the physical dangers from their enemies. The author very strongly is opposed to armed means of responding to our government in today's situation. In what ways, though, should we as American citizenry be on guard?

5   Our founding fathers established means for keeping an out-of-control government in check. What are those means, and how can they be applied? Discuss this from both a government official's perspective and a citizen's perspective.

Chapter Two Six: A Personal Story

1   In what ways did the author feel his close friend was asking the wrong questions about the traumatic circumstances he and his family went through as described in this chapter?

2   What helped sustain the author and his family during the calamities they experienced?

3   The author describes a 'spiritual emergency response team' that stood by he and his family. Can you name an individual or group of individuals who could be on your emergency response team? If not, take some time to consider who could fill in that role. Second: what assistance or skills could you or your family provide to be a part of such a team to help others?

4   To what four things does the author give credit to for being successful in spite of everything in his life falling apart?

5   Having some emotional and spiritual preparation done ahead of time was mentioned as helping getting through a tough time. What do you believe was meant by that and how is that done?

6   What is the main rock solid belief that helped the author's family survive?

7   Key biblical verses memorized ahead of time were of tremendous help in the personal story described in chapter two. Discuss some key verses or principles that you believe will help you get through tough times.

8   What are some characteristics of a survivor?

Conclusions

1. The term 'wall builders' is used several times in this book. What does that mean?

2. What does the author mean by the term 'survivor'? What does he not mean?

3. Glean from every chapter practical attitudes and action steps that will help with the following:

   - What spiritual activities are needed to help make it though tough times?

   - What personal activities do you and your family need to do on your part to help bring your part of your community, state, region or country back to our roots?

   - What group activities are needed to make it through these tough times?

   - What governmental activities need to take place to help restore what we once had as a nation?

   - How will you keep informed and actively engaged in the public arena to effectively and appropriately have an impact in seeing our nation restored?

   - Finally, Biblically speaking, how is God viewing our situation today? Where do you believe He would like us to be?

   - Who would you pick to be a part of your 'emergency response team and why? What skills could you bring to an emergency response team?

   - What is a primary belief statement about yourself that would carry you through tough times? What do you believe in?

   - What traditions do you currently celebrate that help remind you of your personal heritage and also our national heritage. Brainstorm on new traditions and celebrations if you need to add more.

NOTES:

www.ingramcontent.com/pod-product-compliance
Lightning Source LLC
Chambersburg PA
CBHW071244280526
45788CB00004B/1578